G000155396

To my wife

Preface

The purpose of this book has remained the same throughout the life of the first seven editions, namely to provide students (who lack the guidance of any single document embodying the British Constitution) with a full picture in a short compass of the whole area covered by our constitutional law, and to direct their attention towards profitable further study. But in recent years there has been a gradual shift in the balance of constitutional law in practice. The significance of the Commonwealth has diminished to the point where it is no longer essential to consider it, while on the other hand the place of the United Kingdom within Europe and as a member of and contributor to its institutions has become of great importance. Again, administrative law has grown with increasing rapidity as a practical expression of constitutional precepts and demands a more prominent position in a book of this kind.

Now that the time for an eighth edition has come I have therefore taken the opportunity, not just to incorporate the legal developments since 1990, but to rewrite several parts of the book and in the process to reshape it. I have deleted entirely the chapter on the Commonwealth, and have written a new chapter on Parliamentary Sovereignty and the European Dimension. Two former chapters, on the Rule of Law and the Separation of Powers, have been absorbed into other parts of the book where I believe they are better placed. And Part II on Administrative Law has been expanded from its former three chapters into six more substantial chapters.

In the result the book is now a little longer than it was, and to reflect the changes made I have also altered the title. I hope that it provides an up-to-date and balanced introduction to both constitutional and administrative law, and that albeit with an altered title it will continue to fulfil the intentions I first set out in 1960.

DCMY   April 1995
Oxford

Contents

Table of Statutes

List of Cases

xvii

Part I

Principles of British Constitutional Law

Chapter 1

The Nature of British Constitutional Law

It is very difficult to define the term 'constitutional law' as applied to the United Kingdom of Great Britain and Northern Ireland. Naturally it must be that law which is concerned with the constitution of the country.[1] But, whereas in the great majority of the nations of the civilised world it is possible to discover a single document or bundle of documents which embody the constitution of the country concerned, in this country there is no such guide. The provisions of our constitution must be gleaned from among the vast mass of source-material which together forms the whole body of English, Scots and Northern Ireland law. This law is derived partly from custom, but mostly from written sources, namely reports of decided cases, statutes (which, as we shall see in Chapter 2, override any already existing legal rules which conflict with them) and occasionally the writings of jurists, though these latter are only called into account where other guidance for the courts is lacking. The scope of the law is practically unlimited, for it must cover all aspects of the relationships between the individuals and authorities throughout the country. Thus it is inevitable that there should be legal rules concerning crime, matrimonial relationships, real and personal property, conveyancing, wills, sale, civil wrongs, the status of companies, aeronautics and the control of health, to

---

1   It is not intended to explore the meaning of the word 'law' in these pages. This has been the subject of much jurisprudential thought, for which the standard works on jurisprudence should be consulted. Suffice it to say here that law amounts to those rules which the courts of law are bound to enforce.

mention but a few topics. But it is necessary for the constitutional lawyer to divine what, out of the whole mass of the law of the United Kingdom, amounts to part of the constitution.

Hood Phillips has defined the constitution of a state as 'the system of laws, customs and conventions which define the composition and powers of organs of the state, and regulate the relations of the various state organs to one another and to the private citizen'.[2] It is submitted that the constitution of any country must comprise the fundamental structure and organisation of that country, and that therefore constitutional law is its fundamental law, its basic, essential law, whether it be civil, criminal, public or private, together with those rules of conduct laid down to govern the exercise of state power by the official organs of the state. If this postulate is accepted as of general application throughout the world, then it must be accepted for the United Kingdom. It is thus the task of any British lawyer concerned with the constitution to determine which laws out of the whole body of United Kingdom law come within the realm of constitutional law. Since there is no United Kingdom constitutional instrument boldly laying down the laws of the constitution, and showing the lawyer where the line is to be drawn, any assessment of what laws come within the field which is the subject of this book remains largely a matter of personal opinion. It is only rarely that a court of law expresses any opinion on the distinction for, provided the court is able to deduce the law applicable in a given case, it is not often concerned to declare which branch of United Kingdom law it may belong to in comparison with other branches. Sometimes the true classification of a legal rule must remain a matter of doubt, but on the other hand there are frequent occasions when the problem is by no means insoluble. For example, it is a rule of English law that any person who inflicts injury upon another by reason of negligence will be liable to pay damages to that other person, though these damages may be reduced if there has been contributory negligence on the part of the injured

2   *Constitutional and Administrative Law* (7th edn, 1987) p 5.

person. It would be quite possible in the future for Parliament to enact a statute to the effect that contributory negligence should cease to be a defence in an action for negligence, and the effect would be an alteration of one of the branches of the law of torts. But the *method* by which such change had come about (ie parliamentary legislation) would not have been altered at all.

It is not contended that this fundamental law of the state is unalterable. It is normal in most countries that the law of the constitution should provide within itself for the method of its own alteration. Often this is a method quite different from that employed when altering or repealing laws which do not form part of the constitution. To give but one example, the constitutional document of the United States of America provides that any amendment of the constitution may be carried out either by (1) initiation of at least two-thirds of each House of Congress, and ratification by a majority in the legislatures of at least three-quarters of the states, or by (2) initiation of a convention[3] called on the application of the legislatures of at least two-thirds of the states, and ratification by conventions in at least three-quarters of the states, provided in either case that no state, without its own consent, may be deprived of its equal representation in the Senate.[4] These are perhaps fairly complicated methods of change, though only the first method has ever been used, and the position is quite different in this country, where constitutional change may be brought about in the same way as any other change of the law, namely by simple Act of the United Kingdom Parliament.

In many countries the constitution comes into being as the result of a political upheaval, as in the USA, where the constitution which came into force on 4 March 1789 was the political result of the War of Independence. In Eastern Europe after the Second World War the new political masters of most of the Russian satellite countries were able to overthrow the previously existing constitutions, and to

---

3   'Convention' here means a gathering of representatives. It will be seen later that in constitutional law it usually means an important rule of practice, or else, more formally, the title of an international treaty.
4   Constitution of the United States of America, art V.

impose their own will in fresh constitutions. At all events, whatever the executive regime of a particular nation, the constitution inevitably follows from the fact of national political independence. Any such independent country may enact its own laws, including its fundamental laws, for no machinery exists to stop it from doing so. A lawyer is not professionally concerned with politics, and must confine himself to the realms of pure law, but such law is always dependent upon political fact. Jurists have frequently studied the questions of how rules become law, how a constitution comes into being, and who has the power legally to conceive or enact a constitution. But these questions, with which we are not concerned here, must, it is submitted, always remain theoretical, and have little relation to the reality of state necessity and state power. Nevertheless, once a constitution exists, the lawyer must seek to enforce it and to carry it out.

As has been stated above, United Kingdom constitutional law comprises all those laws, derived from the various sources referred to above, which are fundamental to the organisation of the state, together with such lesser rules as are laid down to facilitate the working of the organisation, but it also includes a certain element of pure convention. It must be admitted that there is here a contradiction in terms. Conventions, in the sense of important rules of practice, are mentioned separately because they are not laws, and the courts are therefore not bound to enforce them. They certainly do not amount to law, but they are regarded as being of so fundamental a nature that it would be unthinkable that anyone should transgress them. Also, on the rare occasions when a constitutional convention has been flouted the result has sometimes been that the convention is made into binding law by Parliament.[5] Such conventions may come into being in various ways, but normally they are said to exist because of long usage or of agreement, and because everyone is

5   Eg as happened at the time of the passing of the Parliament Act 1911:
    Chapter 3, below. For recent attempts to ensure that some conventions
    in Australia become binding, see C. Sampford and D. Wood 'Codification
    of Constitutional Conventions in Australia' [1987] PL 231.

entitled to expect that they always will be followed in suitable circumstances.

Because of their practical importance, it may be suggested that constitutional conventions form the very essence or basis of the British unwritten constitution. Instances of these conventions include the rule that the monarch will exercise his (or her) royal prerogative (with a few exceptions) only with the advice of his ministers, and that the ministers of the Crown are collectively responsible to Parliament for the acts of any one of their number in his capacity as a minister. Other important conventions will be mentioned in the appropriate sections of this book. But it may be as well here to note the most basic convention of all, that the government must not flout the generally expressed wishes of Parliament, and that it must not impede the lawful activities of the members of the Opposition. Thus it was that in 1979 the Prime Minister of the day, Mr James Callaghan, advised the Queen to dissolve Parliament so that a General Election could be held. This was after a motion of no confidence in Her Majesty's Government had been carried by a majority of one vote in a specially arranged debate in the House of Commons, the first time that such a vote had been carried in the Commons since 1924. It is because the necessary conventions have not had a chance to grow up gradually that a newly independent Commonwealth country's constitutional document, incorporating the *legal* part of the constitution but not its spirit, may sometimes fail, and even give rise to absolutism.

ENGLISH LAW AND BRITISH CONSTITUTIONAL LAW

The term 'British constitutional law' is used in the title of this present chapter. Yet, as all lawyers are brought up to remember, English law and Scots law are quite different bodies of rules, with distinct traditions and histories, even though in certain fields they have come to bear similarities to each other. Again, the law of Northern Ireland is separate from either of these two systems, and so is that of the Isle of Man and of the Channel Islands. Only between England and Wales has a fusion of laws taken place, although the true reason from which this result followed was the subjugation of the latter country by the former in the middle ages. England, Wales and Scotland together form Great Britain; and Great Britain together with Northern Ireland forms the United Kingdom: this latter body alone is recognised as the state for international purposes. The United Kingdom together with the Isle of Man and the Channel Islands form the British Isles.[6] Each of these countries, other than England and Wales, whose laws and institutions are the same, will be dealt with separately in Chapter 6 below, but for the present it is probably enough to say, in explanation of the phrase used in the chapter heading, that the constitutional laws of England and Scotland have become substantially identical, save in rare instances, and save for nomenclature,[7] and that Northern Ireland, though until 1972 it maintained its own local Parliament and executive, has also been part of the one Union as far as international affairs are concerned,[8] and its laws are for the most part similar to those of England, the powers of any local legislature and executive being subject to those wielded at Westminster. The Channel Islands and the Isle of Man preserve the independence of their laws and institutions more or less intact. The term 'British constitutional law' can be justified in that the principles to be stated in this book are mostly common to England, Wales and Scotland, and are often similar in Northern Ireland, while they have a particular effect upon the Isle of Man and the Channel Islands. It is this common constitutional law which is of significance when considering the home country as the centre of the Commonwealth.

Until the last third of the twentieth century the Commonwealth of Nations (formerly known as the British Commonwealth or, at an even earlier period, the British

6   Strictly speaking the Republic of Ireland also falls geographically within the British Isles, but is now a completely independent country and outside the Commonwealth.

7   Eg *MacCormick v Lord Advocate* 1953 SC 396 (see Chapter 3, below); also the entirely different system of courts (Chapter 6, below).

8   Thus, citizens of the United Kingdom all bear the same nationality and status; see Chapter 7, below.

Empire) was an institution of special constitutional significance, but the various legal links between the United Kingdom and the Commonwealth countries have now virtually disappeared. There remain historic ties between the United Kingdom and the 50 other countries which are full and independent members of the Commonwealth, as well as with the few remaining dependent territories, but the practical co-operation resulting from such ties is largely informal. Even the availability of the Judicial Committee of the Privy Council in London as a court of final appeal from the decisions of Commonwealth courts[9] is no more than an option open to Commonwealth countries if they wish to use it, and in fact the majority of such countries have abolished this right of appeal. For constitutional purposes the significance of the Commonwealth has now been replaced by that of the much more important links of the United Kingdom with European institutions, as will be seen in the next chapter.

THE SUBJECTS COVERED BY BRITISH CONSTITUTIONAL LAW

Although, as has been pointed out above, the identity of the actual rules which come within the scope of our fundamental law may be the subject of dispute, it is submitted that the following short list probably covers the field:

(1) the relationship between the United Kingdom and European institutions;
(2) the law concerning the composition of the national legislature and legislative powers;
(3) the law concerning the composition and functions of central government;
(4) the law concerning the composition and powers of any subordinate or devolved legislature or executive within the United Kingdom;
(5) the hierarchy and status of courts of law;
(6) the limits of personal liberty and the rights of the individual;

9   See Chapter 5, below.

(7) the relationship between the executive and the individual;
(8) the law of citizenship and the status of aliens;
(9) the status of certain national institutions, such as the armed forces and the Church;
(10) the relations between central and local government; and
(11) the law concerning public administration, known as administrative law.

It is on the basis of this list that the remainder of the book will be framed.

FURTHER READING

O. Hood Phillips *Constitutional and Administrative Law* (7th edn, 1987)
E. C. S. Wade and A. W. Bradley *Constitutional and Administrative Law* (11th edn, by A. W. Bradley and K. D. Ewing, 1993)
Sir D. L. Keir and F. H. Lawson *Cases in Constitutional Law* (6th edn, by F. H. Lawson and D. J. Bentley, 1979)
Geoffrey Wilson *Cases and Materials on Constitutional and Administrative Law* (2nd edn, 1976)
O. Hood Phillips *Reform of the Constitution* (1970)
S. A. de Smith and R. Brazier *Constitutional and Administrative Law* (6th edn, 1989)
G. Marshall *Constitutional Theory* (1971)
C. R. Munro *Studies in Constitutional Law* (1987)
H. Calvert *An Introduction to British Constitutional Law* (1985)
D. Pollard and D. Hughes *Constitutional and Administrative Law — Text and Materials* (1990).

Chapter 2

Parliamentary Sovereignty and the European Dimension

I THE SOVEREIGNTY OF PARLIAMENT

Parliament is the primary legislative organ of the United Kingdom, and its most important function is to make laws. Obedience to these laws is obligatory upon all people who owe allegiance to the Crown and who are present within the United Kingdom.[1] In certain respects Parliament has refrained from exercising jurisdiction over the Channel Islands and the Isle of Man,[2] and also at times over Northern Ireland,[3] but it has the right to legislate for the few remaining British dependencies.

It is common to say that Parliament may do anything it wishes, that it is supreme. In law this has been substantially true, and is perhaps the worst fundamental rule of British constitutional law. Until recently the only limitation has been, not of law, but of political expediency, though an element of legal limitation has been introduced since 1973 by the United Kingdom's membership of the European Community, as we shall see presently. Yet parliamentary supremacy only concerns the legislative Acts of Parliament. Only these must be obeyed by courts of law, and no mere resolution, debate or answer to a

---

1 Allegiance does not necessarily depend only upon the possession of British citizenship. The concept of British citizenship is now, in any case, fairly complicated, and will be explained shortly in Chapter 7, below. Again, allegiance does not depend only on residence, but it is sufficient in this chapter to say that allegiance may be either permanent or temporary: the whole problem will be discussed in Chapter 7.
2 See Chapter 6, below.
3 See Chapter 6, below.

question is of any importance as far as the law is concerned.[4] Subject to European Community law, statute law is all-powerful, for it may do anything Parliament wishes; in this sense Parliament is the sovereign body in the land, provided it conforms to the necessary procedure of legislation.

In Anglo-Saxon and Norman times this was not the position. The monarch, as a result of political and factual autonomy, sometimes brought about by conquest, was supreme. He was lord of all land and dispensed all laws. When Parliament was first convened in the course of the middle ages it was with his leave, even though in fact it is possible that he might have found it politically unwise to deny its members the right so to meet. But once Parliament was established as an institution it gradually gained in power and jurisdiction, until in the seventeenth century it became necessary for it to indulge in a trial of strength with the monarchy. It is not within our present purpose to trace in any detail the fluctuations of that struggle, which at its extreme pitch led to the Civil War in the 1640s and the Bloodless Revolution of 1688-1689, but suffice it to say that by the time of that latter event Parliament was triumphant and the monarch was forced to acknowledge its supremacy. It may well be submitted that what had taken place was in fact a political revolution, and that in law nothing could wrest the power of the monarch from him but his own voluntary surrender. This may be so, and the Stuart Kings were not prepared to make such a surrender, but Parliament found the ultimate solution in 1688 by getting rid of the reigning monarch, James II, assuming supreme power, and inviting two new monarchs, William III and Mary II, to occupy the throne jointly, providing they agreed to acknowledge the supremacy of Parliament. In this way the positions were reversed, and the new monarchs reigned by leave of Parliament. In theory there are still a large number of royal prerogatives which may be exercised without recourse to the consent of Parliament, and these will be examined in Chapter 4,

---

4   See, eg, the stand taken by the Court of Queen's Bench in *Stockdale v Hansard*, cited in note 15, p 47, below.

but there is no doubt that any Parliament has the power, if it should so wish, to alter or abolish any such prerogatives which it finds uncongenial, providing such alteration or abolition is carried out by an Act of Parliament and in no other way.

The most important instrument which gave evidence of this newly won sovereignty of Parliament was the Bill of Rights 1689. In origin this was not in fact a statute at all, for it was drawn up at the time when James II had fled the country and no monarch reigned, but William and Mary had to agree to its provisions before Parliament would allow them to assume the throne. Thus no royal assent could be given to the Bill of Rights until it had already taken effect. Its juridical status was validated retrospectively by the Crown and Parliament Recognition Act 1689. A corresponding measure to the Bill of Rights for Scotland was the Claim of Right 1689. As a matter of historical fact Parliament and William reached an amicable agreement, but there is no doubt that Parliament held the whip hand in the negotiations, for it had a throne to give away, but only on its own terms. In particular the Bill of Rights destroyed the power of any monarch to suspend the operation of a law, or to dispense with it in any individual instance, save where such dispensation had not been 'assumed and exercised of late', a loophole by which the prerogative right of pardon was preserved. Again the sole power to levy taxation was finally vested in Parliament, after what had been a long-drawn-out struggle, thus re-embodying and expanding the principle that taxation requires the *consent* of the tax-payers (as now represented by Parliament), which was originally included in Magna Carta 1215.[5] It is this control of the national purse-strings which has made Parliament's position so secure today.

---

5   Magna Carta was not a statute in the sense that is meant today, for it merely set out the demands of the barons to which King John was forced to assent at Runnymede. Nevertheless it has always been treated as having the force and authority of a statute, both by the courts and by Parliament. It therefore must come within the confines of the fundamental law of the land which it is our purpose to discuss in this book.

It may be possible to say that the ultimate real power in any nation rests in its people, who, at least in theory, control their representatives. We might say that a new nation arose in 1689, vesting its greatest power in Parliament, and that a political revolution occurred in 1688-1689, just as it had occurred in 1066 and several times in Lancastrian and Yorkist times, when the identity of the monarch was changed after resort to force. Whatever the cause, from the new order stemmed the new law. Thus our modern constitutional system and law dates from 1689. This we must accept, but the Jacobites would have been the rightful claimants to the throne if it had not been for the Revolution.

Since Parliament from that time has possessed supreme power, it follows naturally that it should be able to retain this power. It is for this reason that Parliament is said not to be able to bind its successors. Although Parliament may pass a statute in, say, 1996, by which it can enact some completely new law, yet it is still within the power of Parliament ten years later, or even only six months later, to abolish or alter that law in any way it thinks fit by a later statute, and such alteration, amendment or abolition may even take place by implication from the later enactments, if it is inconsistent with the former.[6] Perhaps the most striking example of Parliament's power to repeal former enactments is provided by the Irish Free State Constitution Act 1922, which severed that part of Ireland which is now the Republic of Ireland from the rest of the United Kingdom in flagrant violation of the Union with Ireland Act 1800, which had declared the union of the two Kingdoms of Great Britain and Ireland to be 'for ever'. The 1800 Act also provided for the permanent establishment of the United Church of England and Ireland, yet the Church of Ireland was disestablished by the Irish Church Act 1869. It may be that the provision in the Northern Ireland Constitution Act 1973, s 1, that no part of Northern Ireland may cease to be part of Her Majesty's dominions

---

6   As was held in *Vauxhall Estates Ltd v Liverpool Corpn* [1932] 1 KB 733, followed by the Court of Appeal in *Ellen Street Estates Ltd v Minister of Health* [1934] 1 KB 590.

and of the United Kingdom 'without the consent of the majority of the people of Northern Ireland voting in a poll held for the purposes of this section', would be equally ineffective to prevent such severance if ever the Westminster Parliament were determined to carry it through.

In 1971 Salmon LJ put the position graphically in a case in which a Mr Blackburn failed to persuade the Court of Appeal to grant a declaration that the United Kingdom application to join the European Community was illegal because it would be an 'irreversible partial surrender of the Sovereignty of the Crown in Parliament'. Salmon LJ said: 'As to Parliament, in the present state of the law, it can enact, amend and repeal any legislation it pleases'.[7] On the other hand, Lord Denning MR in the same case put the practical realities of the issue into perspective. He said: 'We have all been brought up to believe that, in legal theory, one Parliament cannot bind another and that no Act is irreversible. But legal theory does not always march alongside political reality. Take the Statute of Westminster 1931, which takes away the power of Parliament to legislate for the Dominions. Can anyone imagine that Parliament could or would reverse that statute? Take the Acts which have granted independence to the Dominions and territories overseas. Can anyone imagine that Parliament could or would reverse these laws and take away their independence? Most clearly not. Freedom once given cannot be taken away. Legal theory must give way to practical politics.'[8]

As will be seen in the next chapter, the Parliament Acts 1911 and 1949 have limited the legislative power of the House of Lords in comparison with the House of Commons, and it may be asked whether they have had the effect of binding Parliament for the future as to its procedure in the passage of certain types of statutes. But again the answer must be in the negative, for it is perfectly feasible that Parliament should one day abolish or amend that legislation. Parliament may always at any time legislate

---

7   *Blackburn v A-G* [1971] 1 WLR 1037 at 1041.
8   Ibid at 1040.

for the alteration of its procedure or its own composition, as was done by the Life Peerages Act 1958 and the Peerage Act 1963. It is important, however, to remember that in each case Parliament must act by the composition and according to the procedure which may happen to be legally in force at the time, otherwise it would be possible for some impostor assembly to call itself the true Parliament of the realm. This, after all, is why the courts will not recognise the validity of a mere resolution of either House as law. Nevertheless the internal procedure of each House (as opposed to the relationship between the two Houses) is outside the purview of the courts, for it is within the privileges of the Houses to declare whether or not the proper procedure applicable in any event has been followed. As Lord Campbell once said, 'All that a Court of Justice can do is to look to the Parliament roll: if from that it should appear that a Bill has passed both Houses and received the Royal Assent, no Court of Justice can enquire into the mode in which it was introduced into Parliament, nor into what was done previous to its introduction, or what passed in Parliament during its progress in its various stages through both houses.'[9]

Yet the power of the courts to interpret Acts can sometimes be used in effect to thwart the intentions of Parliament, though the courts do not overtly admit this. Thus in *Anisminic Ltd v Foreign Compensation Commission*[10] the House of Lords was faced with a statutory provision that a decision of the Commission 'shall not be called in question in any court of law'. Yet the Lords held that a determination by the Commission made ultra vires was void, and therefore not a decision at all, so that the court was perfectly free to set it aside. Perhaps this only illustrated how the British doctrine of parliamentary sovereignty is always dependent upon the acquiescence of the courts in it, and shows that it will only remain so long as the courts allow it to remain.

9   *Edinburgh & Dalkeith Rly Co v Wauchope* (1842) Cl & Fin 710. See also more recently the unanimous decision of the House of Lords in *British Railways Board v Pickin* [1974] AC 765, [1974] 1 All ER 609.
10   [1969] 2 AC 147, [1969] 1 All ER 208.

There is, in fact, a great deal of dispute among jurists as to whether Parliament, though always unfettered in areas of legislative jurisdiction, may find itself bound as to the manner and form in which it may legislate. For example, would Parliament be bound by any radical change it might make in its composition, such as by abolishing the House of Lords (as was actually stated in the Preamble to the Parliament Act 1911 to be Parliament's future intention)? Again, it is far from clear whether the undoubtedly sovereign legislature, Parliament, must always remain in its present form. Is it necessary in law for Parliament to be composed of the monarch, the Lords and the Commons, or can the three component parts be differently named and formed, or be reduced in number, as has occurred in New Zealand? Could the monarchy be abolished legally, and a president or head of state put in the place of the monarch? Or would Parliament be bound by any repeal of the Bill of Rights 1689, and fresh subordination of itself to the monarch? A legislative organ is of course necessary in any modern state, if chaos is to be avoided, but it is far from clear whether the British Parliament's legal power to change the law and to legislate upon constitutional matters also includes the power to abolish or change itself radically for the future. The problem will never be solved because any such change would depend for its validity upon the continued support or otherwise of the people, a political and not a legal factor; and jurists would still argue as to whether the new order came into being by law or by political revolution. The past precedents, which include the abdication of sovereignty by the Parliaments of England and Scotland in favour of the new Parliament of Great Britain in 1706, and by the Parliament of Great Britain in favour of the new Parliament of the United Kingdom in 1800, are equally unhelpful for this reason.[11]

---

11 For further reading and the opposing views upon this problem, the following selection of materials might be studied: H. W. R. Wade 'The Basis of Legal Sovereignty' (1955) CLJ 172; H. R. Gray 'The Sovereignty of Parliament Today' (1953-1954) 10 University of Toronto LJ 54; T. B. Smith *Studies Critical and Comparative* (1962) p 1; R. F. V. Heuston *Essays in Constitutional Law* (2nd edn, 1964) Ch 1; G. Marshall *Parliamentary Sovereignty and the Commonwealth* (1957) Pt III and Appendices I-III;

II THE EUROPEAN UNION

After a decade of negotiations the United Kingdom joined the European Community (EC) on 1 January 1973 as a result of the European Communities Act 1972, implementing the Treaty of Accession signed in 1971. The Community, set up by the Treaty of Rome 1957, in fact consists of three communities in number, the European Coal and Steel Community (ECSC), the European Economic Community (EEC), and the European Atomic Energy Community (Euratom), but they share the same institutions. These are the Commission, the Council of Ministers, the European Parliament and the European Court of Justice.

The Commission of the EC is in effect the executive organ of the Community, with its employees drawn from all member states. It is organised into Directorates General and is headed by 20 Commissioners appointed by the governments of the member states for four year terms. All the Commissioners must be nationals of the member states, although not more than two may have the same nationality.

The Council of Ministers is composed of ministers from all the member states, and is the body which enacts legislation. The minister who attends meetings of the Council will on each occasion be the minister responsible in his or her own country for the subject under discussion. There are currently 15 members of the EC, Austria, Belgium, Denmark, Finland, France, Germany, Greece, the Republic of Ireland, Italy, Luxembourg, the Netherlands, Portugal, Spain, Sweden and the United Kingdom.

A. V. Dicey *Introduction to the Study of the Law of the Constitution* (10th edn, by E. C. S. Wade, 1959) Introduction and Pt 1; Sir W. Ivor Jennings *The Law and the Constitution* (5th edn, 1959) Ch IV; Sir D. L. Keir and F. H. Lawson *Cases in Constitutional Law* (6th edn, 1979), Pt 1; M. A. Fazal 'Entrenched Rights and Parliamentary Sovereignty' (1974) PL 295; O. Hood Phillips 'Self-Limitation by the United Kingdom Parliament' (1975) 2 Hastings Constitutional LQ 443; G. Winterton 'The British Grundnorm: Parliamentary Supremacy Re-examined' (1976) 92 LQR 591; P. Mirfield, 'Can the House of Lords Lawfully be Abolished?' (1979) 95 LQR 37; G. Winterton 'Is the House of Lords Immortal?' (1979) 95 LQR 386.

Each member state holds the presidency of the Council for six months at a time, the states following each other in alphabetical order. In practice, therefore, the president of the Council is the head of government or Prime Minister of whichever country is currently entitled to the presidency.

The European Parliament currently consists of 624 members (MEPs) who are directly elected every five years by the electorates of the member countries of the EC: the numbers from each country broadly corresponding with the population size. The Parliament's primary role is to express opinions on the whole range of Community issues and to suggest amendments to proposals coming from the Commission. It is a consultative body which does not have any direct, primary legislative powers, but its views are particularly influential and, in effect, exercise democratic control over the other Community institutions. The Parliament's supervisory responsibilities, particularly through debates, resolutions and the work of its committees, have led in recent years to the adoption of well over half of its proposed amendments to EC legislation. Under the Maastricht Treaty entered into by the member states in 1991, and brought into effect in the United Kingdom by the European Communities (Amendment) Act 1993, the direct powers of the European Parliament have been modestly increased so that it may now amend and even veto certain types of legislation, audit EC expenditure, and has co-authority with the Council for deciding on the EC's budget.

The European Court of Justice rules on the inter-pretation and application of EC laws. Originally it was a single court, but now it sits as a court of appeal, having 16 judges drawn from the member states, at least one being from each such state. There is also a Court of First Instance instituted in 1989 in an effort to spread the load of judicial business of the court which was in danger of building up a serious backlog of work.

According to Community law national Parliaments lose their control over matters entrusted by the Treaty to the Council, though the European Parliament has the power to amend legislation proposed by the Council and the

Commission. The Commission, in its function as executive organ, may make *recommendations* to member states, which are not of binding obligation, but it may also make *decisions*, which are binding upon named addressees, *directives*, which are binding in substance but leave to each member state its choice as to how to enforce them, and *regulations* which, sometimes subject to prior approval by the Council, are directly applicable in each member state. The most important directives and regulations, however, are normally made by the Council, rather than the Commission.

Although the major purpose of the Community was originally economic, it is clear that the powers of the Community organs not only render it necessary in fact for United Kingdom law to conform in some respects with the laws of its European partners, but also make it likely that a certain amount of law will become directly applicable in the United Kingdom from time to time without having been through the normal legislative process in the United Kingdom Parliament. Each House of the Westminster Parliament has established a Select Committee to examine such laws. Inter alia these committees make recommendations as to any amendment of United Kingdom law which may be desirable.

Entry to the EC was envisaged by most member states as the first stage in a process of possible European political integration, and this was taken further by the provisions of the Single European Act, signed in Luxembourg and The Hague in 1986, which came into force on 1 January 1993, and was implemented by the United Kingdom by the European Communities (Amendment) Act 1986. The Single European Act provides that the Community shall be an area 'without internal frontiers in which the free movement of goods, persons, services and capital is assured'. The Maastricht Treaty, which came into force in 1993, sought to build upon this by providing, inter alia, for more inter-governmental co-operation in foreign affairs and defence, police, environmental protection, progress towards a common European citizenship, and the aim of a common European currency. The abolition of most customs and immigration controls between EC countries proved popular for citizens generally, but some of the Maastricht objectives were controversial. The British government had already opted out of a provision in the Maastricht Treaty for common social legislation governing workplace affairs, and the European Communities (Amendment) Act 1993 includes the necessary provisions for enabling the United Kingdom to move only slowly upon some of the other objectives.

It is certainly intended by some member states within the EC that the Community shall in due course become a single federal country, but it seems unlikely that this will come about in the foreseeable future, even though the EC under the provisions of the Maastricht Treaty is now subsumed into what is called the European Union (a term intended to indicate the co-operation between member states on such matters as foreign affairs and police). One particular provision in the Maastricht Treaty would appear to work against such progress. There has in recent years been some feeling that Community laws have been intruding too much upon minor matters of mainly local significance only. Accordingly the notion of 'subsidiarity' has been included in the Treaty. Subsidiarity lays down that European laws are only to be made when they are more effective than national legislation. Thus the principle has been accepted that decisions affecting the lives and conduct of the citizen should be taken as close to the individual affected as may be reasonably possible. The Maastricht Treaty also set up a broadly based Committee of the Regions. It has only advisory status, but must be consulted by the European Commission and the Council of Ministers on an extensive range of policies affecting regional issues.

Nevertheless Community law overrides national laws. Does this therefore mean that our Parliament has surrendered some portion of its sovereignty in favour of the Community institutions? Of course Parliament will undoubtedly usually want to do its best to conform with Community legislation, but successive Lord Chancellors have stated that it would remain within the power of Parliament to repeal by a subsequent Act any former Act applying a treaty which had been made. Under the powers enacted by the Referendum Act 1975, the first national consultative referendum was held throughout the United Kingdom, in which the electorate was asked to vote 'Yes' or 'No' to a question whether the United Kingdom should stay in the European Community. In the event there was a convincing majority for the answer 'Yes'. But the very asking of the question suggests that a contrary vote might have led to a later Bill to repeal the European Communities Act 1972. It can be argued that a specific Act passed later by the United Kingdom Parliament which is directly in conflict with Community legislation would have to be followed by British courts. Sorting out the result of such a clash would then be a political, rather than legal, matter for the government, and it may well result in later amending United Kingdom legislation. However it has now been made clear by the courts that the provision in s 2(4) of the European Communities Act 1972 directing the courts to apply Community laws has the effect of precluding them from applying any earlier municipal law which is inconsistent with Community law.[12] Thus in *Macarthys Ltd v Smith*[13] the rules of Community law entitling women to equal pay with men were held by the Court of Appeal to be applicable in preference to inconsistent provisions in the Equal Pay Act 1970. Again the House of Lords held in 1990 that it was obliged to set aside any rule of municipal law which infringed a provision of EC laws.[14]

The view of the European Court of Justice is that member states have limited their national sovereignty. Yet this very primacy of Community law is the result of the provisions of the European Communities Act 1972, which

---

12   And see F. M. Auburn 'Trends in Comparative Constitutional Law' (1972) 25 MLR 129; D. G. T. Williams 'The Constitution of the United Kingdom' [1972B] CLJ 266; cf F. A. Trinidade 'Parliamentary Sovereignty and the Primacy of European Community Law' (1972) 35 MLR 375; Sir Leslie Scarman 'The Law of Establishment in the European Economic Community' (1973) 24 Northern Ireland LQ 61; E. Ellis 'Parliamentary Supremacy After a Decade of EC Membership' (1982) 7 Holdsworth LR 105; O. Hood Phillips *Constitutional and Administrative Law* (7th edn, 1987) pp 74-82.

13   [1981] QB 180, [1981] 1 All ER 111.

14   *R v Secretary of State for Transport, ex p Factortame Ltd* [1990] 2 AC 85.

could always be repealed or amended by a later Act of Parliament. So far as basic constitutional law is concerned, therefore, entry to the European Community may not in itself be so fundamental a change as it seems at first sight.

III THE COUNCIL OF EUROPE

The Council of Europe, which is quite different from the EC, is a rather looser organisation open to membership by all countries within Europe. In the course of time it is intended that several other countries will become members of the EC, and it may well be that one day there will be efforts to integrate the EC and the Council of Europe, but that will be a long time in the future. For constitutional purposes the most important institution of the Council of Europe is the Court of Human Rights.

Along with most other countries in the continent the United Kingdom has accepted the competence of this court, and acceded to the European Convention on Human Rights signed in 1950. This enables the legality of a United Kingdom Act of Parliament to be challenged before the court by any other state (since 1951) and by any private individual (since 1966) on the ground that it conflicts with a specific fundamental human right set out in the Convention, provided that the legal process within the United Kingdom has been exhausted. There is thus now the possibility of some external, though not internal, judicial review of United Kingdom Acts.[15]

Decisions of the Court of Human Rights are, however, not directly enforceable within member states, even though since 1993 it has become a full-time court with an enhanced remit. So a finding that any United Kingdom legislation is in breach of the European Convention still requires the passage of amending legislation at Westminster to become

15 As in *Golder v United Kingdom*, decided by the European Court of Human Rights on 21 February 1975, [1975] Yearbook of the European Convention on Human Rights 290. It is perhaps unfortunately confusing that under the Maastricht Treaty the European Court of Justice now has new and binding competence over human rights questions, but this is of course only upon issues falling within EC law.

effective. Later legislation of this kind cannot be guaranteed because the United Kingdom government and Parliament may not necessarily be prepared to follow the Court's ruling. Such a reaction is rare, but it did occur in the passage of the Prevention of Terrorism (Temporary Provisions) Act 1989. This makes temporary provision, inter alia, for the arrest and detention of people on reasonable suspicion of involvement in the commission, preparation or instigation of an act of terrorism. The Court of Human Rights had in 1988 held by a majority that such detention for up to seven days, as provided in earlier temporary anti-terrorist legislation, conflicted with the European Convention, and that it should not exceed four days. Nevertheless the 1989 Act retains the seven days' maximum period, subject to review of the detention order by a magistrate after four days.

IV SOVEREIGNTY IN SCOTLAND

A final word should be said about the status of parliamentary sovereignty in Scotland, for although it has been beyond question for England, Wales and Northern Ireland, it has been doubted in a case in Scotland so far as that country is concerned. In that case, *MacCormick v Lord Advocate*,[16] the use by Queen Elizabeth of the numeral 'II' was disputed, primarily for the very commonsense reason that although Elizabeth I had been Queen of England she had never been Queen of Scotland, and that there had never before been a Queen of Scotland known by that name. The use of the numeral ever since the Queen's accession in 1952 had been authorised by the Royal Titles Act 1953, for that statute allowed Queen Elizabeth to use whatever numeral she thought fit in the United Kingdom. But it was alleged that the Treaty of Union between England and Scotland declared that any law inconsistent with such of its terms as were declared in the Treaty itself (and the subsequent Acts of the Parliaments of England

---

16 1953 SC 396; and see similar doubts in *Gibson v Lord Advocate* 1975 SLT 134.

and Scotland) to be unalterable was void, and therefore that it forbade the use of the numeral in this way. It was ultimately held by the Court of Session in Edinburgh that the Treaty did not actually forbid the use of the numeral, and that the petitioner had in any case no legal title or interest to sue, but there were nevertheless dicta to the effect that had the 1953 Act been repugnant to the Treaty, then the later Act would have been void unless it was generally approved in Scotland. It is far from clear in the dicta whether the sovereign body for Scotland is really the whole people (presumably expressing their will by plebiscite, which had never before been held there), but in any event some of the judges in the case considered that the Treaty and Acts of Union gave no express jurisdiction to the Scottish courts to determine questions concerning conflicts between future Acts of the United Kingdom Parliament and the Acts of union.

It is not suggested that the Treaty is so fundamental as to be totally unchangeable, for statutory alterations have been made before,[17] but on those occasions the changes have never been challenged in the courts, and apparently must possess the approbation of the people. The solution to this puzzle is still unknown, though an application to the European Court of Human Rights would now seem feasible. We may be sceptical as to the validity of the special Scots law rule today. In a case of 1872 a challenge to the validity of the Royal Assent to the Irish Church Disestablishment Act 1869, as being inconsistent with the Coronation Oath and the Act of Settlement 1700, was rejected on the ground that an Act of Parliament is superior in authority to any court of law, and accordingly no court is competent to question its validity.[18] At any rate, with this possible, but unclear, exception for Scotland, the principle of parliamentary sovereignty in the United Kingdom remains probably the most basic tenet of our constitutional law.

---

17   Eg by the Universities (Scotland) Act 1853, which enacted that professors at Scottish universities need no longer be members of the Presbyterian Church of Scotland.

18   *Ex p Selwyn (Canon)* (1872) 36 JP Jo 54.

FURTHER READING

J. A. G. Griffith, M. Ryle and M. A. J. Wheeler-Booth
Parliament: Functions, Practices and Procedures (1989)
Sir G. Slynn *Introducing a European Legal Order* (1992)
T. B. Smith 'The Union of 1707 as Fundamental Law'
[1957] PL 99, reproduced in *Studies Critical and
Comparative* (1962) p 1
D. Lasok and J. W. Bridge *Institutions of the European
Community* (5th edn, 1991)
P. S. R. F. Mathijsen *A Guide to European Union Law* (6th
edn, 1994).

Chapter 3

The Working of Parliament

We have examined the extent of Parliament's sovereignty in the previous chapter. Other important functions include discussion of policy and surveillance of the government. In this chapter it is necessary to consider five aspects of Parliament, namely the composition of Parliament, the duration of Parliament, the procedure for making laws, other functions of Parliament, and parliamentary privilege.

I COMPOSITION OF PARLIAMENT

There are three component parts of Parliament, the monarch, the House of Lords and the House of Commons. It is more usual to regard Parliament as composed of only the two Houses which sit at Westminster, but it is strictly correct to consider all three elements as part of the whole, for no legislation can come into being without the participation of the monarch, as will be seen presently. The institution of the monarchy itself will, however, be examined in Chapter 4 rather than in the present chapter.

THE HOUSE OF LORDS

The House of Lords is the successor of the old *Curia Regis*, which comprised the King's advisers, but the House itself, as a gathering of all the noblemen of the land, probably stems from sometime in the thirteenth century. One great difference between the modern House of Lords and the

27

Curia is that the latter was a feudal body, whereas feudalism now plays no part in our law or society. The membership of the House has altered comparatively little since earliest times, though there have been several recent modifications. At present there are about 1200 people qualified to sit in the Lords, though many do not exercise their right to do so. Membership is comprised as follows:

The Lords Temporal

These may be subdivided into:

(1)   all hereditary peers and peeresses of the realm, except Irish peers. This group does not include heirs to peerages who merely hold courtesy titles and are not in fact the head of their line.[1] Peers in their own right include dukes not of royal blood, marquesses, earls, viscounts and barons, and they currently number about 775.[2] Under the Peerage Act 1963, however, it is now possible for any peer to disclaim his peerage for the duration of his life, leaving his next heir to decide whether or not he also will surrender the peerage when the time comes for him to succeed to the title. The main purpose of this new function is to enable those who wish to sit in the House of Commons, if duly elected, to escape the automatic disqualification (mentioned below) which attaches to a peer. Under a Standing Order of the House of Lords a procedure has also been established whereby peers who do not wish to attend the House regularly may obtain, or even sometimes be assumed to have obtained, leave of absence. Although this cannot legally prevent a peer from sitting whenever he so desires, it does nevertheless have this practical effect, thus discouraging the occasional attendance in the legislature of noble 'backwoodsmen';

(2)   all life peers created by the monarch, under the terms

1   Irish peers, and all persons who possess courtesy titles, rather than peerages, are eligible to sit in the House of Commons, if elected: see below.
2   In February 1994 there were 774, but the number is gradually reduced by extinction of title whenever a peer dies without an heir. In addition 12 peerages had been disclaimed for life under the Peerage Act 1963.

of the Life Peerages Act 1958. Any man or woman may receive the rank of baron under this Act, which was passed as a step towards reform of the composition of the House. Objection may be raised that in fact the government of the day may nominate its own supporters as life peers, but it seems that at present none of the major political parties are likely to abuse the power conferred by the Act, which has been used partly to boost the Labour benches in the Lords, and partly to give seats in the chamber to people eminent in diverse walks of life. In February 1994 there were 403 life peers, 60 of them women;

(3) the twelve Lords of Appeal in Ordinary ('Law Lords'), who are life peers appointed under the terms of the Appellate Jurisdiction Act 1876, as subsequently amended.[3]

The Lords Spiritual

These are the Archbishops of Canterbury and York, the Bishops of London, Durham and Winchester, and the 21 most senior other diocesan bishops of the Church of England, according to seniority of appointment. The Bishop of Sodor and Man, however, never has a seat in the House, as he is always a member of the Tynwald of the Isle of Man.[4]

There are, however, certain disqualifications which will prevent a peer from being able to take his seat in the House, although he would otherwise have been entitled to do so. These disqualifications apply to:

(1) aliens;
(2) peers under the age of 21;
(3) persons convicted of treason;
(4) members expelled by the House acting as a court of law,[5] unless pardoned; and
(5) bankrupts.

3 The Act of 1876 originally provided for the appointment of only two Lords of Appeal in Ordinary.
4 See Chapter 6, below.
5 A peer expelled by a resolution of the House of Lords acting as a legislative body cannot be excluded permanently. The judicial functions of the House will be discussed later in Chapter 5.

The Speaker of the House of Lords is the Lord Chancellor, who is also a member of the government, and is not therefore expected to be impartial in party matters.[6] The political parties maintain supporters in the House, each party having its Leader, but since the peers do not become members of the House by election as party candidates there are many peers who have no political affiliations at all. The Conservative Party has often been able to rally sufficient support to ensure a majority in any critical debate or measure, though this power has been affected by the modern practice of appointing life peers, as shown above. But in any case, as we shall see when examining the functions of Parliament, party politics play a much smaller role in the Lords than in the House of Commons. In the Queen's Speech at the opening of Parliament in 1967, the Labour Government stated its intention to initiate legislation to reform the House of Lords still further, and this intention was reaffirmed in 1968, but the Parliament (No 2) Bill, which was designed to achieve such a reform, had to be abandoned in 1969 because of determined opposition from a number of back benchers on both sides of the House of Commons.

The Labour Party Conference in 1977 voted over-whelmingly for total abolition of the House of Lords, and in 1988 for its replacement by an elected chamber. This latter object is in the current revision of Labour's objectives if and when they come back to power. On the other hand a review committee set up by the Conservative Party reported in 1978 in favour of retention of the House with a reformed composition, consisting of two-thirds elected and one-third nominated members. Many other schemes for reform of the composition of the House of Lords, and sometimes of its powers, have been put forward from time to time; and there is a general recognition that the present composition is very difficult to defend in a modern democratic state, however well the House may do its work in practice. It seems realistic to expect eventual reform, though not abolition, of the second chamber.

6   The Lord Chancellor need not strictly be a peer, but according to modern practice he always is, even if this involves the special conferment of a peerage upon him on appointment to his office.

THE HOUSE OF COMMONS

The House of Commons, sometimes known as the lower House of Parliament, is a representative assembly. Its history dates from <u>the thirteenth century</u>, and the methods of providing representatives to sit in the House have altered very greatly in the course of its existence, particularly as a result of the Reform Acts of the nineteenth century. Today there are 651 members of Parliament (MPs), and each is elected by universal adult suffrage in one of the parliamentary constituencies in the United Kingdom. The total number of MPs has been recently increased, partly because of an increase in the representation at Westminster from Northern Ireland (effected by the House of Commons (Redistribution of Seats) Act 1979, consolidated by the Parliamentary Constituencies Act 1986), and partly as a result of the regular redistribution of the seats currently for Great Britain. Under the provisions of the Boundary Commissions Act 1992 such redistribution takes place more frequently than hitherto. This Act is intended to ensure that the next General Election after 1994 will be based on new constituencies. The whole of the Kingdom is divided into these constituencies according to roughly equal groups of population.

There is no limit to the number of candidates who may offer themselves for election in each constituency, though each must deposit £500 with the returning officer of the constituency, and this sum will be forfeited by the candidate if he fails to poll at least one-twentieth of the total votes cast. The great majority of candidates belong to political parties, the most powerful of which are the Conservative, Labour, Liberal Democrat, Official Unionist, and Scottish and Welsh National Parties, and successful candidates will support or oppose the government party according to their affiliation. But in law a candidate's or member's affiliation to a party is ignored: his status as a member of Parliament alone, if he is elected, is all that is recognised.[7] The electoral system is commonly known as

7   The existence of political parties is, however, apparently assumed by the terms of the Ministers of the Crown Act 1937, and the post of Leader of the Opposition is recognised in that statute.

'first past the post', in that the candidate who gains the highest individual number of votes in an election is successful. This can on occasions mean a victory by only a very few votes more than the candidate gaining the next highest number of votes, and often by a minority of the total votes cast. Some argue that there should instead be a system of proportional representation, but the current system does have the arguable virtue that the House of Commons usually ends up with one political party having an overall majority of members, thereby providing a more stable support for the government of the day.

Anyone may 'stand for Parliament',[8] but the following persons are disqualified from sitting in the House:

(1)   aliens;
(2)   persons under the age of 21;
(3)   those convicted of treason or serving a term of imprisonment or detention for more than one year. (If an MP is sentenced for any other offence to a period of imprisonment the Speaker must be informed, but the member is not expelled from the House unless a motion to expel him has been passed.);
(4)   certain persons suffering from mental illness;
(5)   peers and peeresses in their own right, other than the holders of Irish peerages;
(6)   clergy of the Church of England and the Church of Ireland, ministers of the Church of Scotland, and priests of the Roman Catholic Church. Although none of these churches is represented directly in the Commons, the Church of England is represented, as has been seen, by its bishops in the Lords. Clergy of the Church in Wales may, however, sit in the Commons as a result of the Welsh Church Act 1914;
(7)   bankrupts;
(8)   anyone guilty of corrupt or illegal practices at parliamentary elections. These terms are statutorily defined, and the consequences of disqualification are

8   Under the Representation of the People Act 1981 those disqualified from election to the Commons because they are serving a term of imprisonment or detention for more than one year are also disqualified from being nominated for election.

dealt with in the House of Commons Disqualification Act 1975;

(9) judges of the Supreme Court of Judicature and the Crown and County Courts, and stipendiary magistrates;

(10) civil servants, police officers and members of the armed forces on the active list;

(11) sheriffs, and returning officers as regards the constituencies of which they are returning officers;

(12) members of non-Commonwealth legislatures; and

(13) holders of certain specified offices, listed in s 1 of and Sch 1 to the House of Commons Disqualification Act 1975.[9] These are usually offices of profit, but the Act also preserves the traditional method whereby an MP may resign from the House, namely by applying for one of the sinecure positions of Steward of the Chiltern Hundreds or of the Manor of Northstead.

The chairman of the House is the Speaker, who is elected from among its members by the whole House at the beginning of each Parliament. The election is often unanimous after the government party and the Opposition have held informal discussions upon the subject.[10] The political division of the members is far more pronounced than in the House of Lords. The government, headed by the Prime Minister, is normally formed from the party which has the largest group of members in the Commons, and which then becomes known as the government party. The Prime Minister will appoint an influential member of this party as Leader of the House. Members of parties which oppose the government party are then termed the Opposition, and the most powerful Opposition party will elect one of its number to be Leader of the Opposition. The support of members of either the government or Opposition parties in any vote is ensured by the means of the 'Whips', who are MPs chosen within the party concerned, or by the Prime Minister for the government party, to maintain party discipline and regularity of attendance at the House

9   The House of Commons Disqualification Act 1975 also lays down that no more than 95 members may hold ministerial office.

10   The election was contested in 1951, 1970 and 1992.

on important occasions. Although 'Whips' also function in the House of Lords their importance is not so great there, partly because of the large number of independent members in that House, and partly because, as we shall see presently, the Lords have far less power than the House of Commons. Government 'Whips' hold titular posts as Lords of the Treasury or members of the Royal Household. The strict party system in the Commons may in some measure detract from the quality of debate in that chamber, and it does tend to prevent members from voting according to conscience; but on the other hand the stability, both within the House and of the government — for, as we shall see in the next chapter, the existence of the government depends on the continued support of the majority in the Commons — contributes greatly to the general stability of the country, and enables the House to work through a lot of business without undue hindrance.

II DURATION OF PARLIAMENT

Section 7 of the Parliament Act 1911 enacts that no Parliament may last for more than five years, and unless Parliament has already been dissolved by the monarch its life will terminate by lapse of time exactly five years after it came into being. A General Election of members of the Commons will then be held, although the composition of the Lords will not be altered by this event. It is, however, always open to Parliament to extend its own life by means of an Act of Parliament, and this has been done, for example, during the war of 1939-1945; but it is conventional to effect this prolongation only from year to year. Casual vacancies in the Commons are filled by holding a by-election in any constituency affected.

Each new Parliament is summoned by the monarch, and divides its time into sessions, normally covering periods of about one year each, though they are sometimes held more frequently. Sessions are ended by the monarch 'proroguing' Parliament. The sittings of Parliament within each session are also divided up by periods of 'recess'.

III PROCEDURE OF MAKING LAWS

A law is made by the passing of a statute through Parliament. In the course of its passage it is known as a Bill, but when it is passed it becomes an Act of Parliament. Such Acts must be approved by a majority of the votes cast in each House, and then receive the assent of the monarch. Certain exceptions to this procedure of the passage of a Bill through both Houses are provided for in the Parliament Acts 1911 and 1949, which will be discussed later in this chapter. There are three main kinds of Bill: Public, Private and Hybrid. Public Bills concern law which will be of general application when it is passed. Private Bills are measures dealing with personal matters or local matters in a certain area of the country only. Hybrid Bills are otherwise Public Bills which nevertheless affect private interests in such a way as to render it desirable that part of the procedure for Private Bills be adopted for their passage. The procedure for the passage of each of these types of measure will be sketched in these pages, but first it should be noted that such procedure is conventional only, save where the Parliament Acts 1911 and 1949 apply. It is within the competence of either House to vary its procedure, yet the conventional practice is unlikely to be disturbed. Bills will be either Government Bills (that is, introduced by a member of either House who is also a minister) or Private Members' Bills (introduced by a member of the House who is not a member of the government, or who is introducing the Bill purely in his private capacity as a member of the House). Government Bills occupy far more time in Parliament, because parliamentary time is allocated by the Leader of the House, and very little time is allotted to Private Members' Bills. In fact only certain Fridays of the year are currently set aside for this purpose, and members wishing to introduce such Bills must ballot for the right to do so on one of these days. It may be thought that in practice too little time is now allowed for the consideration of Private Members' Bills, which are often of greater importance than the time spent on them would suggest. They do indeed provide the ordinary citizen with the opportunity to initiate legislation which is not necessarily of importance to the government. Such measures were the far-reaching Matrimonial Causes Act 1937, introduced by Mr (later Sir) A. P. Herbert, the Murder (Abolition of Death Penalty) Act 1965, introduced by Mr Silverman, and the Local Government (Access to Information) Act 1985, introduced by Mr Robin Squire.

PUBLIC BILLS

These Bills may originate in either House, although most Bills in fact go through the Commons before the Lords, and Money Bills and other Bills with financial clauses may not originate in the House of Lords, but the procedure is largely similar in both Houses. The member introducing the Bill will either present it at the Table of the House or, more rarely, move for leave to introduce it.[11] In either case the member will previously have given notice of his intention. There then follow at intervals the first and second readings, the committee stage, the report stage and the third reading. The first reading is purely formal, when the Clerk of the House reads out the title of the Bill only. The second reading, however, is the vital stage at which it is decided whether a Bill will be defeated out of hand or will go forward for further consideration. Normally the member who introduced the Bill will speak in its favour, pointing out the main principles involved. There is no possibility of altering details at this stage, and the Bill must stand or fall on its general merits. If the Bill is unopposed, then it will be 'read' a second time very quickly, but if it is opposed then a debate on the principles of the Bill will take place, after which a vote is taken. Of course a Government Bill is very unlikely to be defeated, but a Private Member's Bill is by no means as certain to be approved at this stage, as voting is rarely on party lines. In 1965 an alternative procedure for the second reading of Public Bills in the Commons was introduced, whereby a minister may move

---

11   Private members also have the privilege of moving for leave to introduce Bills after 'Government business' on any day, but as only ten minutes are allowed for each such introduction, plus ten minutes for any opposition, little more than publicity is likely to result.

that any such Bill be referred to a standing Second Reading Committee, consisting of from 30 to 80 MPs, which shall then report to the House, with reasons, whether or not they recommend that the Bill be read a second time. The procedure may not be used if at least 20 members rise in their places to object to the minister's motion. But if a Bill is sent to the Second Reading Committee, the report of the Committee must be put to the House for a vote without amendment or debate. This has resulted in a saving of parliamentary time, and the passage of many non-controversial Bills for which the government would not otherwise have been able to find debating time. Since 1979 all Private Members' Bills have automatically been referred to the Second Reading Committee. Another reform introduced at the same time, and also aimed at time-saving, was the limitation of speeches in Second Reading debates in the Commons to ten minutes.

If the Bill is defeated at its second reading it is then withdrawn, but if it is approved by a majority of the voters in the count it goes on into the committee stage. In this stage a committee of the House, whose membership is allotted in the proportion that the parties have in the House, or in some cases a committee consisting of the whole House, will consider the detailed provisions or clauses, as they are called, of the Bill. In the consideration of a very long Bill time limits sometimes have to be set for this stage,[12] but usually the committee is able to discuss and alter if necessary any part of the Bill it thinks fit. At this stage the party majority of the government is not so important, as voting is not upon the general principles of the Bill, now accepted, but merely upon how best to formulate the detailed provisions throughout the Bill. In 1980 the Commons began the experiment of sending certain Bills for their committee stage to a Special Standing Committee. The main advantage of this has been that such a committee has been given the power to hold

---

12 The 'Kangaroo' (only certain amendments are chosen for debate); the 'Guillotine' (a time limit is placed on the debate of each part of a measure); and the 'Closure' (an overall time-limit is placed on consideration of the Bill). These methods are not confined, however, to debate in committee.

sittings at which evidence may be taken from outsiders, thus going some way towards the committee stage practice for Private Bills, mentioned below. After the committee stage is over, the committee reports to the whole House what it has done. At this, the report stage, it is still possible for the House to amend the Bill, but this is not often done in practice. Finally the Bill receives its third reading, when a last debate is held upon the general principles of the measure. Again it is possible for the Bill to be defeated, but if it has already passed the other stages, particularly the second reading, it is most unlikely that this will occur. As far as details are concerned it is usual that only amendments of slips in the wording of the Bill are made. Once it has passed the third reading it has 'passed the House'. In 1967 the House of Commons' Select Committee on Procedure made recommendations designed to cut out waste of time and repetition of debate in the report stage and third reading of Public Bills, and as a result these last stages have for many Bills now been largely combined in practice.

Having been approved in one House, the Bill must now go to the other House and pass through similar stages in the course of the same session of Parliament. If the Bill should be approved in the second House in the same form in which it eventually passed the first House, then it will be sent forthwith for the Royal Assent, and will become an Act of Parliament. If on the other hand it is approved in principle, but altered in some respect in its details, then it will be returned for further consideration in the first House. If the amendments of the second chamber are then agreed to in the first chamber the Bill will go for the Royal Assent, but if no such agreement can be reached after a reasonable time the Bill was, up till 1911, treated as defeated, just as if the second House had rejected the Bill outright. The Parliament Acts of 1911 and 1949 have, however, altered this position greatly, and the effect of these Acts will be considered after the procedure for other types of Bill has been discussed.

PRIVATE BILLS

Private Bills are either local or personal. Local Private Bills for the most part concern some particular locality in the country, and are usually initiated by local authorities, whereas personal Private Bills deal with the affairs of certain particular persons or estates. Not all personal Bills, however, are necessarily Private Bills, and, for example, personal Indemnity Bills are usually Public Bills. Local Bills may be considered first in either House, but personal Private Bills must go through the Lords before the Commons. In each House the stages of the Bill are for the most part similar to those employed in the case of Public Bills, but a major difference appears in committee, for at that stage any interested party at all may appear and oppose the Bill, and witnesses may be called, so that the procedure takes on a quasi-judicial aspect. In addition the members of the committee who conduct this inquiry must be entirely disinterested in the affairs concerned in the Bill. This procedure is the outcome of a desire to protect the interests of those affected parties whose causes would not be likely to excite public interest. Once a Private Bill has passed one House it is unlikely to be altered or opposed in the other, though this does occasionally occur. After passing both Houses, the Bill goes for the Royal Assent.

HYBRID BILLS

When a Hybrid Bill is under consideration the opportunity for interested parties to appear at the committee stage must be given, but otherwise the procedure adopted is similar to that where a Public Bill is under consideration. Thus the members of the committee need not be disinterested.

In the case of all Bills the Royal Assent is required before they become law. Sometimes a Norman-French formula is used to signify the assent, though it is not customary now for the monarch to assent in person. But the assent is usually just notified to each House by the Speaker of the Commons and the Lord Chancellor respectively, under the powers provided in the Royal Assent Act 1967.

The Parliament Acts 1911 and 1949

From the foregoing account it will be seen that originally it was possible for either House to veto the legislative endeavours of the other by refusing to pass Bills sent to it from the other. Convention had it that the non-representative chamber, the Lords, should not so obstruct the Commons if the Commons had become set upon the passage of a particular measure, but nevertheless the Lords broke this convention several times during 1908 and 1909, when the Commons had a huge Liberal Party majority. After two general elections and considerable political rancour and bitterness, the government prevailed upon the Lords to allow a Parliament Bill to pass the upper chamber, by holding over it the promise of the King that he would if necessary create a sufficient number of new peers who would support its passage. The provisions of the resulting Parliament Act 1911 were altered even further to the detriment of the power of the Lords by the Parliament Act 1949, which was passed under the procedure laid down in the Act of 1911. The procedure provided for in the two Acts is as follows:

(1)   in the case of a *Money Bill* having passed the Commons, it shall receive the Royal Assent without the approval of the Lords unless it has been passed by the Lords within one month of being sent to the Lords, provided that the Bill was sent to the Lords at least one month before the end of the session. This, therefore, strengthens the previous constitutional convention that financial Bills should only begin in the Commons, and should not be altered by the Lords. The Acts provide guidance for the Speaker of the Commons as to what Bills are properly to be regarded as Money Bills, but the Speaker is nevertheless legally empowered to certify any Bill as a Money Bill in theory, for the Acts provide that the Speaker's certificate to this effect is final and cannot be questioned in any court of law;

(2)   the power of the Lords to reject any Bill attempting to extend the maximum duration of Parliament

beyond five years is left unimpaired;
(3) in the case of any other *Public Bill* the power of the
Lords to obstruct the wishes of the Commons by
rejection, complete or partial, has been severely
curtailed. Under the provisions of the Acts, if a Bill
has been passed in the Commons and then rejected
in the Lords, and in the next session of Parliament it
is again passed by the Commons, but the House of
Lords does not also pass it without amendments
(except amendments approved by the Commons), the
Commons is empowered to send it up for the Royal
Assent despite the Lords' opposition. It is also
provided that at least one year must have elapsed
between the second reading of the Bill in the
Commons in the first session and the third reading
in the Commons in the second session. When this
procedure has been adopted because of the Lords'
opposition to a Public Bill, the Speaker of the House
of Commons must endorse the Bill with a certificate
that it has been passed by the Commons according to
the procedure laid down in the Parliament Acts before
it is sent up for the Royal Assent. Again this certificate
is final.

It will be noted that the Acts do not deal with Private
Bills, and therefore the power of the Lords to veto Private
Bills if the House should so wish is left untouched. The
Lords no longer has any practical power over Money Bills
at all, and theoretically it would be possible for the Speaker
to certify any Bill as a Money Bill, though an abuse of this
authority would very probably have disastrous political
repercussions. It is in any case most unlikely in the British
parliamentary system that the Prime Minister would be
able to persuade the Speaker to take such a step. The
delaying power of the Lords over other Public Bills, with
the one exception of Bills to extend the life of Parliament,
is now just one year. Under the Act of 1911 it was two
years, and this cutting down of the time was the raison
d'être of the 1949 Act. The Parliament Acts make clear the
Commons' control over public finances, and they assert the
supremacy of the Commons over the Lords, though of

course it would always be open to any Parliament to alter the position by future legislation. This is, however, most unlikely to occur so long as the Lords remains basically an hereditary chamber. One of the reasons why the parties have found it so difficult to formulate an agreement on the basis of which to reform the composition of the Lords has been that such agreed reform might have to carry with it an increase in the actual power of the second chamber. This largely explains the general opposition of the Labour Party to most schemes so far suggested. Although there is at present a permanent Conservative majority in the Lords, the Labour Party has often been reasonably content with this state of affairs because it is a largely powerless majority in any case of real conflict. The Parliament (No 2) Bill had to be abandoned in 1969 partly because so many MPs could see the impracticability of the clauses in it designed to reduce still further the Lords' power to delay legislation. Yet any reformed and reinvigorated House might be less helpless against the wishes of a resolute Commons. But there have been a number of clashes between the government and the Lords in the past 30 years, and it is thought likely that some further effort to reform the House of Lords may be made in the near future.

It is, however, fair to add that the House of Lords has rarely intended to be obstructive during the past 80 years, and that the Lords' amendments to Bills are more often accepted by the Commons than rejected. The peers only rarely vote on strict party lines, and it may be asserted that the passage of the Parliament Acts in a sense proved to be the saviour of the upper House. Once it is clear that their will cannot prevail over the Commons, the efforts of peers in the discharge of their parliamentary functions have naturally become more consistently constructive. The only time that the procedure for passing a Public Bill without the consent of the Lords has been invoked since 1949 was in the passage of the War Crimes Act 1991. It is suggested that the House of Lords now exercises much more usefully than in former times those functions which the members of the famous Conference of 1917-1918, presided over by Lord Bryce, considered ought to be discharged by the second chamber. These functions are the examination and revision of Bills first dealt with in the Commons, the delaying of Bills for so long, and no longer, as may be needed to enable public opinion to be expressed upon them, the initiation of less controversial Bills which can be expected to pass through the Commons fairly easily, and the full and free discussion of important matters for which the Commons may not immediately be able to find time. A recent authority has asserted that the House of Lords is the best second chamber in the Commonwealth, and one which stands comparison with its counterparts in almost any developed country.[13]

IV OTHER FUNCTIONS OF PARLIAMENT

It would be a great mistake to think of Parliament only as a legislative assembly. In fact legislative business occupies only about one-half of the time taken by the sittings of Parliament. Nevertheless it is the legislative business and power of Parliament which is of importance to lawyers, who are only concerned to discover and to apply law; and it is only when legislating that Parliament is responsible for the creation of law, as the term legislation itself would imply. It is therefore not necessary to elaborate here upon the other functions of Parliament, but, in order to aid a full understanding of Parliament, which is a deliberative as well as a legislative assembly, the most important of them at the present day will be listed:

(1) general debate, which may take place in either House upon any subject it deems fit to examine. There is no necessity for there to be any vote upon a motion, but often such a vote does take place, and frequently along party lines. Some of the subjects chosen for debate are put forward by the government, and others by the Opposition, for the time of Parliament is allotted by the Leaders of each House partly to matters the government wishes discussed and partly to subjects chosen by the Opposition. Here, as in the second and

13   S. A. de Smith *Constitutional and Administrative Law* (5th edn, 1985) p 310. This view has been modified in later editions of the book.

third functions mentioned below, it can be seen that Parliament, or at least the House of Commons, acts as a bridge between the people and the government, through the agency of the people's elected representatives;

(2) questions may be addressed by any member, usually to a minister, upon any subject connected with the administration of public affairs for which the minister or member is officially responsible, providing that it does not concern proceedings pending in Parliament. Often the questions are suggested by constituents. It is obvious that unless a proper answer of a more or less satisfactory nature is made the subject is likely to give rise to some agitation. It may be noted here that one of the salient differences between the procedure of the United Kingdom Parliament and that of the United States Congress is that there is no 'question time' in the latter, largely because members of the government do not sit in Congress;

(3) the making of ministerial statements, which may or may not be followed by debate;

(4) work in committees. This is often upon Bills, as has been seen above, but it may be upon matters of any kind referred for inquiry to a committee by the House. The Public Accounts Committee and the Select Committees on Estimates and on the Nationalised Industries for many years played an important part in keeping a check on the administrative process. In recent years Parliament has experimented with the introduction of other committees to investigate broad fields of administrative activity, and in 1979 the House of Commons reorganised its committee structure in order to gain much more control over the main functions of government. There are now 20 select committees (and four sub-committees) of the House, each charged with one of the main areas of government, such as defence, foreign affairs, home affairs, the Treasury and the Civil Service, etc. The committees are small, ranging in numbers from eight to eleven, and there is also a 'liaison' committee, consisting of the chairmen of these committees, which

resolves all demarcation disputes between the committees. The general opinion is that the powers of these committees to interview and question ministers, who are normally prepared to attend on request, and then to report upon their findings have had a salutary effect in shifting some of the control of the executive arm of government back to the elected representatives of the people in the Commons. Occasionally joint committees of the two Houses sit for the purpose of discussing matters of common concern, and in particular there is a joint committee to consider all Bills covering statute law revision and the consolidation of previous enactments;

(5) the consideration of the privileges of the two Houses, which will be discussed more fully below;

(6) the House of Lords, but not the Commons, is also the highest court of appeal for England, Northern Ireland and, in civil cases only, for Scotland. This topic will be discussed in Chapter 5.

V PARLIAMENTARY PRIVILEGE

In order that members of both Houses may carry out their tasks without undue interference or fear, certain privileges have attached to them since very early times. The historical reason for their existence is that Parliament is strictly the 'High Court of Parliament', and superior courts of law maintain similar privileges which protect them in the exercise of their judicial functions. Although they are mainly similar in each House, for the privileges belong essentially to Parliament as a whole, there are some differences in effect. The privileges common to members of both Houses are:

(1) freedom of speech in debate from any outside interference at all. This privilege has been undoubted since the ultimate triumph of Parliament over Stuart despotism in the seventeenth century, and forms Article 9 of the Bill of Rights 1689. The meaning of 'debate' appears to have been widened considerably,

for this privilege covers also communications between members or made to members by their constituents upon parliamentary business. Such missives would therefore be immune from any operation of the law of libel, as they are considered by the House to be 'proceedings in Parliament'. A recent limitation upon the meaning of the phrase and upon this privilege which has been imposed by the House of Commons itself will be discussed below;

(2)   freedom from arrest during sessions of Parliament and for 40 days before or after a session. A peer, however, remains permanently covered by this privilege. But it is not as wide as it may seem, for it probably only covers civil arrest, now practically unknown. It is still debatable whether a member of either House is privileged from arrest for summary offences, though the absence of authority upon the point shows its comparative practical unimportance. A Select Committee on Parliamentary Privilege recommended, in 1967, the abolition by statute of freedom from arrest so far as members of the House of Commons are concerned, though it has not yet been implemented;

(3)   the Commons have the right of access to the monarch through the Speaker, whereas each peer has theoretically the right of individual access, probably very rarely exercised;

(4)   each House has the right to regulate the qualifications for its membership, subject to any statute which may have been passed on the subject, and to regulate its own internal proceedings. Thus, much of the foregoing account of procedure in the passing of Bills is a matter upon which the courts cannot inquire;

(5)   the right to impeach, that is, to try any person for any offence in the House of Lords, with the Commons acting as prosecutors. This appears now to be obsolete, not having been exercised for nearly 200 years, and its abolition was in any case recommended by the select committee in 1967. But impeachment is still a live possibility in the United States, where article II, s 4 of the constitution provides: 'The President, Vice-

President and all Civil Officers of the United States shall be removed from Office on Impeachment for, and Conviction of, Treason, Bribery, or other High Crimes and Misdemeanors'. In 1974 President Nixon became the first US President to resign office when the House of Representatives Judiciary Committee voted overwhelmingly to recommend to the House that he be impeached;

(6) the right of each House to punish for breach of privilege or contempt of the House. The privileges are those listed in this chapter, but contempt may in theory be anything which offends the dignity of the House. Whether anything amounts to a contempt or a breach of privilege is for the House itself to decide, and the courts have no cognisance of such a problem, except in the one instance where either House punishes a person, as for example by imprisonment, for a breach of privilege, but gives a patently bad reason for doing so. On a subsequent application for habeas corpus[14] the court may declare the proceedings to be unlawful,[15] but if no reason for the claim of the House should be given it would be impossible for any court to interfere.[16] Punishment awarded by the

14   See Chapter 7, below.
15   See, eg, *Stockdale v Hansard* (1839) 9 Ad & El 1. There a report of prison commissioners contained a libel of Stockdale, and the Commons had ordered the parliamentary printers, Messrs Hansard, to publish the report for sale to the public. In the subsequent libel action by Stockdale, Hansard, under instructions from the Commons, pleaded that the report had been published by order of the House, and that it was therefore covered by parliamentary privilege. The court held that this was not one of the privileges of the House. Freedom of speech covered papers passed between members themselves, but not those allowed to pass into the hands of the general public.
16   As occurred in the *Middlesex Sheriff's Case* (1840) 11 Ad & El 273, which was the sequel to *Stockdale v Hansard*, above. The Commons had passed a resolution that the publication of reports etc was essential for the proper functioning of Parliament, and that the House had the sole right of judging the validity and extent of any privileges claimed. The House allowed the damages to be paid in Stockdale's case, but made it clear that any future attempt to bring such an action would itself amount to a contempt of the House. Nevertheless Stockdale proceeded to bring another similar action against Hansard, and judgment was given in Stockdale's favour in the absence of any plea by the defendant, but when the Sheriff of Middlesex

House may be by imprisonment, fine (at present this is only possible in the Lords), reprimand, admonition or, in the case of a member of the House, expulsion. Legislation has been expected for some years to give the Commons power to impose fines, and also to abolish the power of either House to imprison, but it has not yet materialised. The most common recent instances of the privilege to punish being exercised are concerned with contempt by journalists, and with disorderly behaviour in the House. In 1991 the House of Commons resolved that the failure of the two sons of Robert Maxwell to answer questions put to them in a hearing by the Social Security Select Committee of the Commons was a contempt of the House, though no punishment was exacted.

In addition to the above each House has certain other privileges. The Commons maintains the right to control finance and initiate financial legislation. Originally this was mere convention, but the existence of the privilege has been strengthened by statute in the Parliament Acts 1911 and 1949, as described above. The Commons also claims as a privilege that the Crown will place the best construction on its deliberations, a privilege now of no practical importance. The additional privileges of the Lords are more numerous, but of very little real importance. They include the right to summon judges for advice on questions of law (in practice now never exercised, because of the presence in the House of the Lords of Appeal in Ordinary since the Appellate Jurisdiction Act 1876),[17] exemption

levied the damages awarded in this latter case, and he refused to give the sum back when so ordered by the Commons, he was forthwith imprisoned by order of the Commons for contempt and breach of privilege of the House. Although the Sheriff applied for habeas corpus, his application failed because the Speaker's warrant of committal did not contain any reason for the allegation of contempt or breach of privilege. Ultimately the Parliamentary Papers Act was passed in 1840 to make law the very extension of privilege which the Commons had claimed, and the Sheriff was set free when the session of Parliament ended shortly afterwards. The enactment of the statute may perhaps be regarded as an act of conscience by the Commons.

17   The judges were last summoned in an English appeal in *Allen v Flood* [1898] AC 1, and in a Scottish appeal in *Free Church of Scotland (General Assembly) v Lord Overtoun* [1904] AC 515.

from jury service, and the right of any peer alone to enter a protest against any measure of the House in its Journals.

A final word on the subject of parliamentary privilege as a living issue should be said. The original reason for the existence of the privileges, that is to protect the *High Court* of Parliament, has practically disappeared, for, except where the House of Lords acts as a final court of appeal, the real functions of Parliament are now those of debate and legislation. It cannot any longer be the case that all the existing privileges are necessary to protect members in the discharge of their duties. In particular it may be argued that the power to punish should be transferred from the Houses themselves to the courts of law, so that the Houses may no longer seem to be judges in their own cause. Indeed it is possible that only the safeguarding of freedom of speech actually inside Parliament is now necessary to ensure the existence of a free and virile assembly. In the present state of the law, however, it is to be expected that members will not claim privilege frivolously or unless there is real need to do so. The record of the House of Lords in this respect has in modern times been good, and it is extremely rare today for any peer to claim privilege. On the other hand the Commons has in the present century acquired a certain notoriety for its eagerness to claim and assert privilege. A standing committee of the house, the Committee of Privileges, meets whenever needed to consider alleged cases referred to it and to advise the whole House upon its proper course of action. Divers activities of individuals outside the House may be held by the House to amount to contempt,[18] and the courts of law are powerless to decide otherwise.[19] Often the cases alleged are not really infringements of the necessary freedom of the House, but merely instances where MPs have felt annoyed about things said of them.[20] Public feeling has on occasions

18   Eg *R v Paty* (1705) 2 Ld Raym 1105, where five Aylesbury men had brought an action against the returning officers for refusing their votes at an election. They were committed to prison by order of the Commons for breach of privilege.

19   Eg *Middlesex Sheriff's Case* (see note 16, p 47, above).

20   Eg the offence taken by MPs at the comments in the *Sunday Express* upon the methods of allocating petrol ration coupons: 563 HC Deb 407 (1957).

been roused by what one may well consider abuse of the essential privileges of the House. It is a subject which has been much canvassed in letters to newspapers — the writers themselves having been in danger of the wrath of the Commons! But the general public and the courts can work no changes or diminution in the power of the House. It is therefore for the House itself to use these powers with discretion and good sense; the virtue of the preservation of freedom should not be permitted to turn into the vice of tyranny. It was encouraging that one 8 July 1958,[1] the House decided by a small majority that a letter written by a member to a minister was not necessarily a 'proceeding in Parliament', thus rendering the writer immune from the law of defamation. Mr George Strauss MP had written a letter to the Paymaster-General, who represented the Minister of Power (a peer) in the Commons. In it he alleged that the London Electricity Board had behaved in a scandalous manner in the way in which it invited tenders for the purchase of its scrap metal. The contents of the letter were disclosed to the Board, which, after some exchange of correspondence, informed Mr Strauss that it intended to sue him for libel. Although Mr Strauss claimed that this was a breach of the privileges of the House, a claim which was supported by the Report to the House of the Committee of Privileges, this claim was rejected on a free vote in the House. The status of such letters in the future will depend upon their actual nature, and their writers will only be absolutely privileged where the contents can be truly considered to pertain to parliamentary business, or the duty of the writer as a member of one of the Houses of Parliament.

It is perhaps worth noting that, as a result of a subsequent official inquiry into the activities of the London Electricity Board, it was found that no such irregularities as had been alleged in Mr Strauss's letter had in fact taken place. The present indications are that MPs since the Strauss affair have been more circumspect about claiming that their privileges have been infringed,[2] and in 1967 the

1   591 HC Deb 208.
2   See D. C. M. Yardley 'The House of Commons and its Privileges since the Strauss Affair' (1962) XV Parliamentary Affairs 500.

Select Committee on Parliamentary Privilege, set up by
the Commons, recommended a number of changes in
procedure to reduce the publicity attendant upon
complaints of breach of privilege, and to cause the House
to use its penal jurisdiction more sparingly. In order to get
rid of the false impression of members of the Commons as
a 'privileged class', the Committee further suggested that
the term 'privilege' should be replaced by that of 'rights and
immunities'. But this Report has yet to be fully
implemented, though Standing Orders on resolutions of
the House have introduced some of the more minor
recommendations. In 1977 the Committee of Privileges
itself recommended that the term 'proceedings in
Parliament' should be defined by legislation for the purpose
of absolute privilege, but again parliamentary time has not
yet been found to implement the recommendation. As late
as 1993 the Speaker of the Commons made a statement
in the House reminding the courts of the Commons'
freedom of speech in debate, and warning them not to
attempt to infringe it.

FURTHER READING

Sir William R. Anson *The Law and Custom of the
Constitution* Vol 1: Parliament (5th edn, by M. L. Gwyer,
1922)
Sir Thomas Erskine May *The Law, Privileges, Proceedings
and Usages of Parliament* (21st edn, by C Boulton, 1989).

Chapter 4

The Executive

The executive is the organ of state which is responsible for carrying out the law and performing the routine administration of the country. Until the seventeenth century, as has been pointed out above in Chapter 2, the authority for this exercise of power derived from its own strength and ability to coerce opposition, but since that time it has exercised its powers with the authority of Parliament. Traditionally the monarch is the all-powerful part of the executive, but from earliest times he has acted with advisers, and since the subordination of the executive power to that of Parliament these advisers have become so much more important that in fact they are now the active members of the executive, while the monarch is usually only informed of decisions made and actions carried out or to be carried out. An example of this principle in practice is the custom of the Chancellor of the Exchequer to inform the monarch of his Budget proposals each year on the day before he is due to introduce them into the House of Commons. But the executive is still in law referred to as 'the Crown', and this has become a collective term to cover not merely the monarch but the whole body of his advisers and their servants. The Crown thus symbolises the central government. It is correct to classify the Prime Minister as part of the Crown, and just as correct so to place the most junior of Inland Revenue officials and all members of the armed forces.

For convenience the component parts of the Crown or executive may be stated to be:

(1) the monarch;
(2) his ministers;
(3) the central government departments, staffed by the civil service; and
(4) the armed forces.

Cutting across this division, as far as 1, 2 and 3 above are concerned, is the Privy Council, which is also part of the Crown. Its nature will be explained in due course in this chapter.

I THE MONARCH

The monarch is the King or Queen Regnant for the time being and holds the position of head of state. Throughout this book the term 'monarch' is used to describe the person of the head of state in the United Kingdom, for it is thought to be more definitive than 'King' or 'Queen', which may appear to refer to a particular monarch, or 'sovereign', which may be confused with parliamentary sovereignty. Succession to the monarchy is hereditary under the terms of the Act of Settlement 1700, as amended by the Union with Scotland Act 1706, the Union with Ireland Act 1800, and His Majesty's Declaration of Abdication Act 1936. Under these statutes the heirs of Sophia, Electress of Hanover, who was a granddaughter of King James I, were to succeed to the throne according to rules similar in most respects to those governing feudal descent of land, provided that no heir may succeed to the throne unless he or she is in communion with the Church of England. The present Monarch is Queen Elizabeth II. Provision is made by the Regency Acts 1937-1953 for the appointment of a regent if the monarch should be below the age of 18 years or seriously ill, and for counsellors of state if the monarch should be absent from the realm.

II THE MINISTERS OF THE CROWN

The monarch's advisers are often collectively termed 'the government', though this phrase is misleading, for in theory the whole of the Crown is the government. They are, however, the most vital members of the government, for they are responsible for the formulation of executive policy. As the Crown carries out its functions under the control of Parliament, it has become a convention of the constitution that the ministers should be drawn from the political party with a majority in the House of Commons, or occasionally from any coalition of parties which hold such a majority. The continuation in power of any particular government depends upon the continued support of Parliament, or, more particularly, of the Commons, and thus the legislature and the executive are closely dovetailed in the British Constitution. The monarch has the right to choose his Prime Minister, who will in turn choose the other ministers with the approval of the monarch. This right of the monarch is, however, of little real importance, as the continuation in office of the ministers will depend upon the support of a majority in the Commons which is unlikely to be forthcoming unless they are acceptable to such a majority. The stated practice of the Labour Party is to elect a leader who alone would be supported by the party as Prime Minister, and in 1965 the Conservative Party adopted a somewhat similar practice.

The Prime Minister, with the consent of the monarch, usually appoints to ministerial office members of either House of Parliament. Most of the ministers will be members of the Commons,[1] and the rest by convention sit in the Lords. In the rare case of the Prime Minister appointing as minister someone who does not sit in either House it is usual for that person to be created a peer. It is customary that the heads of the more important ministries should be members of the Commons, so that they may explain or defend themselves and their policies in the House where the elected representatives of the people are

---

1   The House of Commons Disqualification Act 1975 limits the number of ministers who may sit in the Commons to 95.

assembled. It now appears to be a convention for the Prime Minister himself to be a member of the Commons, rather than of the Lords,[2] and the Chancellor of the Exchequer must perforce sit in the lower House, which alone is concerned with financial affairs. It is not our present purpose to provide a detailed list of the ministers, for such a list would contain the names of over 100 different offices. A few examples of those at present in existence should suffice. Among the more important offices are those of Lord Chancellor, Chancellor of the Exchequer, Secretary of State for Foreign and Commonwealth Affairs, and Home Secretary. All such ministers are the heads of different government departments, which in the case of the offices just quoted are respectively the Lord Chancellor's Department, the Exchequer, the Foreign and Commonwealth Office and the Home Office. Among lesser ministers are, eg, the Attorney-General, Ministers of State in various departments (who may be regarded roughly as second ministers in such departments), Parliamentary Secretaries and Under-Secretaries of State. Although all such officials are members of the government, a small inner group of the more important ministers is called the Cabinet, which meets frequently under the chairmanship of the Prime Minister or, if he or she is absent, a deputy appointed by the Prime Minister, and very probably formulates most government policy, only consulting junior ministers as and when it seems appropriate or desirable. It is impossible to say with any certainty what does take place in Cabinet meetings, as they are very secret and no publication of their transactions is allowed for many years. Again, the government normally provides a display of unanimity concerning its policies, both in Parliament and outside. Any disagreement is ironed out in private, or else, as sometimes occurs, any ministers who cannot accept the majority view will resign from office.

2 Most writers assert that this practice has the status of a convention, as the last Prime Minister who sat in the Lords was Lord Salisbury (1895-1902). It may be noted that the Earl of Home was appointed Prime Minister in 1963 while a member of the Lords, and he did not renounce his peerage under the Peerage Act 1963 until four days later. He was then a member of neither House of Parliament for some two weeks until he had successfully fought a by-election for a seat in the Commons.

The one major exception to this rule was provided in 1975 when the government consciously permitted ministers to express different views, and even to campaign actively for them, before the referendum in June upon whether or not the United Kingdom should remain a member of the European Community. It is generally considered that future governments will not wish to follow this precedent, though the government allowed a free vote in the Commons for its members on the European Assembly Elections Bill in 1977.

III THE CENTRAL GOVERNMENT DEPARTMENTS

All the departments of the Crown which are concerned with the government of the country are termed Central Government Departments, and each is headed either by a minister or, in the case of non-political departments, such as that concerned with inland revenue or with customs and excise, by a permanent head or commissioner. Although the Ministers will change whenever a government changes, the permanent officials will not, and even in the political departments there will always be an official, designated as Permanent Secretary, at the head of the permanent staff, who will see that his minister's policy is carried out. The permanent staff are all members of the civil service, a body of permanent Crown servants recruited into the service as a career, though legally only holding office at the pleasure of the Crown. At the present time steps are under way, as a result of government policy, to create executive agencies to run various governmental functions on business lines, and some 60% of all civil servants have now been moved to these semi-independent agencies. The result would seem to be a much-reduced central civil service.

As in the case of the different ministers, it is not intended to detail all the Central Government Departments. The ambit of the work of most will be self-evident, as in the case of, for example, the Ministry of Defence, the Foreign and Commonwealth Office, and the Department of the

Environment. Perhaps a word should be said here about the departments of the Lord Chancellor and of the Law Officers, as these are of particular interest to lawyers. The Lord High Chancellor of Great Britain is Keeper of the Great Seal and presides over the House of Lords both as a legislative assembly and as a final court of appeal.[3] With the help of his department he selects all puisne judges of the High Court, Circuit Judges and Recorders, who are then formally appointed by the Crown on his advice, and he appoints and removes all Justices of the Peace, except those in the Duchy of Lancaster who are appointed and removed by the Chancellor of the Duchy of Lancaster.[4] In addition he is responsible, with the aid of his department and of the English Law Commissioners,[5] for advising on questions of law reform. The Law Officers are the Attorney-General and Solicitor-General for England and Wales, and the Lord Advocate and Solicitor-General for Scotland. The English Law Officers are usually members of the House of Commons, and the Scottish Law Officers may be, though in recent years one or other of the Scottish Law Officers has often been a member of the House of Lords, and sometimes one of them has been a member of neither House. Their responsibilities differ slightly, but in the main they represent the Crown in civil litigation in England (including Wales) and they may prosecute in both England and Scotland in criminal cases of great importance or gravity, especially murder cases. The English Law Officers hold positions as the head of the Bar, and thus have some authority in questions of professional etiquette, though most questions of this kind are dealt with by the Bar Council in London or by the Faculty of Advocates in Edinburgh. The Head of the Scottish Bar is the Dean of the Faculty of Advocates. The Law Officers advise other

3   On this subject see Chapter 5, below.
4   The nature of these various judicial offices will be explained in Chapter 5, below.
5   The Law Commissions Act 1965 establishes two Commissions, one for England and Wales, and the other for Scotland, responsible respectively to the Lord Chancellor and to the Lord Advocate and the Secretary of State for Scotland, and with the duty to review the law with a view to its systematic development and reform, including preparation for codification and the repeal of obsolete and unnecessary Acts.

government departments on points of law. They or their deputies may intervene in litigation where the interests of the public would require such a course to be taken, for they are the representatives of the public interest where public rights are at stake.

All government departments will have powers and duties conferred upon them by Acts of Parliament, and these may in turn be supplemented by powers acquired under the Royal Prerogative, which will be examined later in this chapter. Although in the past it was more useful for statutes to confer powers upon the monarch, it is now common to find statutes conferring such duties or powers upon ministers or departments direct and by name. In view of the majority support in the Commons which any government should be able to command, and which it must command in order to remain an effective government, it may be that the government does from time to time have a tendency to dictate to Parliament by telling it what it intends to do and relying on its party majority to carry through its proposals. Thus, although Parliament still in theory maintains the whip-hand over the executive, in practice the reverse may sometimes be more true. Where this is so the result may sometimes be regrettable, but it cannot be denied that inevitably it gives rise to strong government in a way unknown in, for example, France for many decades before the establishment of the Fifth Republic in 1958, for there the multiplication of political parties led to the necessity of a succession of coalition governments. The Italian Parliament since the Second World War has also been a monument of instability, giving rise to the formation and collapse of over 50 governments in less than 50 years, though it is hoped that legislation in 1993 to reduce the use of proportional representation in elections, and to move a good way towards the British method of elections, will bring more stability.

Although there is a danger of the British government acting in a highhanded way occasionally, yet the legal sovereignty of Parliament is always present, and no government would be able to try the patience or conscience of its own customary supporters too far without finding an incipient rebellion on its hands. In the 1992-93 session of

Parliament the government had very great difficulty with some of its supporters during the passage of the European Communities (Amendment) Bill, and only secured its enactment after several near-defeats.

IV THE PRIVY COUNCIL

The Privy Council has a far longer history than the present Cabinet or government system. It dates from Anglo-Saxon and early Norman origins, and was an earlier body of advisers of the monarch. Although the present Cabinet has really usurped this ancient position of the Privy Council, the older body has never become entirely obsolete, and it still has some important functions. Appointment to the Council is still technically by the monarch himself, although membership is now partly conventional and partly arranged according to the wishes of the government of the day, with the one distinction that members are appointed for life. The conventional members are:

(1) the Lord President of the Council, who normally presides at any of the Council's meetings, and who is in any case a member of the government for the time being;
(2) the Archbishops of Canterbury and York;
(3) the Speaker of the House of Commons;
(4) all present and former Cabinet ministers, but not other members of the government; and
(5) the Lords of Appeal in Ordinary, the Lords Justices of Appeal, the Lord Chief Justice, the Master of the Rolls and the President of the Family Division of the High Court.

Other persons who from time to time attain the rank of Privy Councillor, as and when the monarch or the government decide on such appointment, are usually leading statesmen from other Commonwealth countries, or distinguished persons from any walk of life.

The purposes of the Privy Council today are several, but it only meets as a full body (about 300 Privy Councillors are usually living at any one time) on the death of the monarch, when it will make all arrangements for the funeral, accession and coronation that may be necessary. This meeting of the Council is sometimes known as an Accession Council. Otherwise the meetings of the Privy Council are always in small bodies or as committees. The most important function is that of making Proclamations or Orders in Council. Proclamations may be made under the Royal Prerogative, to be explained later in this chapter, usually on the advice of the Prime Minister. Orders in Council are largely made under statutory powers, and will be considered more fully in Chapter 10, below. Committees of the Council sit for various purposes, such as to deal with constitutional issues concerning universities and colleges, to direct research in certain fields, and to hear appeals from other countries within the Commonwealth.[6]

V THE ARMED FORCES

All members of the Royal Navy, Army and Royal Air Force[7] are servants of the Crown, and thus these services may be regarded as being parts of the Crown. The powers of the armed forces and their members are controlled partly by Acts of Parliament direct and partly through certain prerogative powers of the Crown. All members of the armed forces are dismissible by the Crown at will, and at common law no action will lie at the suit of a serviceman against the Crown for arrears of pay, or for wrongful dismissal or the refusal of a pension after service ceases,[8] unless such a pension has been fixed by statute.

6   In the Judicial Committee of the Privy Council: see Chapter 5, below.
7   This is not an exclusive list, for these services are now divided up in many ways. The principles cited in this section cover all members of the regular armed forces, including, for example, the Royal Marines. The former separate women's services are now integrated into the men's services. The various reserve and auxiliary forces are also included. The Home Guard, which no longer exists as an armed force, was in the same position, and doubtless would be again if ever it were reconstituted.
8   See, eg, *Grant v Secretary of State for India* (1877) 2 CPD 445. The position has not been affected by the Crown Proceedings Act 1947, which will be discussed in Chapter 12, below.

VI THE DOCTRINE OF THE SEPARATION OF POWERS

Three basic and essential functions in the administration of any independent state are legislative, executive and judicial. From a realisation of this generally accepted opinion has sprung at various times and in different countries the idea that the agencies through which these functions are exercised should be kept separate from each other, the intention being to prevent the concentration of more than one of the powers in any single authority, which might lead to tyranny, and to make sure that the due exercise of each is in no way hindered by the agencies responsible for the other two. Theories concerning the best methods of carrying out this intention go back as far as Aristotle, and find expression in the constitutions of many nations, although in no country is the doctrine practised in such a way as to render the three functions entirely exclusive.

The Constitution of the United States of America, which came into effect on 4 March 1789, probably provides us with the most extreme example of a practical separation of the three fundamental powers.[9] It is based upon a mistaken interpretation by the French writer Montesquieu of the position in England in the eighteenth century,[10] though it should be added that the founding fathers were interested in Montesquieu's views as applied to America, and they were in no way concerned about whether or not he had interpreted the English Constitution of his time accurately. The first three articles of the United States Constitution vest federal legislative powers in Congress, the executive power in the President, and the judicial power in the Supreme Court of the United States. These powers appear to have been intended for the most part to be mutually exclusive, so that no member of one branch of

9   The Constitution of the State of Massachusetts may possibly be more extreme in some respects.
10   *De l'Esprit des Lois*, Ch VI, paras 3-6. In fact, as Madison pointed out in *The Federalist*, Montesquieu was mainly concerned to warn against the dangers of monopoly of power, and he may therefore have been less mistaken than is sometimes asserted.

government may be a member of either of the others as
well, but even so the separation was not complete, and
various 'checks and balances' between the three agencies
were provided. Thus, the President is empowered to veto
legislation of Congress, and such a veto may be overridden
by a two-thirds majority in each House of Congress. Any
treaties which the President enters into with other
countries must be ratified by a two-thirds majority in the
Senate before they may come into effect. Although the
normal rule is that no member of the government may also
be a member of Congress, yet the Vice-President ex officio
presides over the Senate, and may if necessary exercise a
casting vote, as he did twice in 1993. The President
nominates judges to office in the Supreme Court (though
approval of such a nomination must be given by the Senate
before a nominee may assume office, and approval is
sometimes withheld), and finally, even though there is no
provision for this in the Constitution itself, it has been
found essential that the Supreme Court should have the
power to declare Acts of Congress (or of any state
legislature) or actions of the President illegal if they should
in any way transgress the provisions of the federal
Constitution.[11] The system in the United States has justly
been described as a separation of powers modified by
checks and balances.

In the United Kingdom it is clear that the three
fundamental powers exist, just as they exist in other
countries. Two have already been described, and the third
will be considered in the next chapter. The legislative
power is vested in Parliament, the executive power in the
Crown, and the judicial power in the courts of law. It is
part of the object of this book to point out both the existence
of these basic functions and also their essential differences
in nature, but there is much overlapping between them and
between the authorities in which the powers are vested.
It is therefore appropriate to summarise the principal
factors which in the United Kingdom render it impossible
to insist that any strict separation of powers exists. It is

11   For a short but stimulating discussion of this topic, see Learned Hand
     The Bill of Rights (1958). See also Chapter 5, below.

necessary in part to refer forward to certain material
included in the later chapters of the book, but it is probably
best to provide a complete picture of the position at this
earlier stage:

(1) members of the government are usually members of
one or other of the Houses of Parliament, because it
is desirable that all ministers of the Crown should be
held responsible to Parliament for their actions. This
is not an absolute rule, as may be seen from the case
of Sir Frank Soskice, who was defeated in his
constituency at the 1950 general election, but
nevertheless retained his ministerial position as
Attorney-General, being elected to the Commons in
a by-election when another member of the Labour
Party stood down from his own seat; or of Mr Gordon
Walker, who became Foreign Secretary in the Labour
government which came to power in 1964, despite his
own defeat at the general election of that year, and
who only resigned that office after his defeat at a later
by-election. Probably a member of the government
may retain his office providing he does not cease to
be a member of one of the Houses of Parliament for
more than a few months. It is, however, more usual
for any minister who takes office without possessing
a seat in either House to be created a peer so that he
may sit in the Lords. It may be noted that one of the
most useful methods of checking upon the activities
of ministers or of the government as a whole is the
parliamentary question: there is no such parallel
possibility in the United States, where members of the
government do not sit in Congress and there is no
'question time'. The concept of ministerial responsibility to Parliament has been copied in the
constitutions of most independent Commonwealth
countries;

(2) the monarch, who heads the government, also in effect
forms the 'third House of Parliament'. Both this point
and the last one lead to the common usage of
'Parliament' and 'government' as interchangeable
terms, although such a practice is of course incorrect.

It will be recalled that the government, through its parliamentary majority, holds the whip-hand in the House of Commons, and thus can usually force legislation through that House, and ultimately through Parliament as a whole;

(3)   the monarch is the 'fountain of justice', being technically present in all his courts of law, responsible for many judicial appointments, and exercising the prerogative of mercy in respect of persons convicted in the courts. Thus he plays a part in all three of the fundamental powers;

(4)   Parliament is strictly called the 'High Court of Parliament' and, although the House of Commons carries out no judicial functions today, the House of Lords is still the ultimate court of appeal. The Lords of Appeal in Ordinary sit in the House of Lords both as a legislative body and as a court, and they are also Privy Councillors, as is indeed the Speaker of the House of Commons. The Lord Chancellor also plays a part in all three of the powers, being a member of the House of Lords as a legislative body and as a court, responsible for a number of judicial appointments, and also a member of the government;

(5)   although the independence of the judiciary is in practice jealously preserved, superior judges are appointed by the Crown or by the Lord Chancellor, and are removable by the Crown on an address by both Houses of Parliament to the Crown, while inferior judges are appointed and removable by the Lord Chancellor;

(6)   the power to make delegated legislation is usually vested by Act of Parliament in the government;

(7)   administrative tribunals, as well as many of the ordinary courts of law, are created either directly by Act of Parliament or by delegated powers conferred upon ministers by statute. Their powers and duties may be both judicial and administrative;

(8)   Justices of the Peace are primarily judges, but still retain certain administrative duties, such as licensing;

(9) local government powers are created by Parliament
or by Royal Charter and are both legislative and
executive within the district of each local authority.

Enough has been said to show the interrelation between
the three fundamental powers. It is very probable that the
overlapping of powers and authorities insures against
arbitrariness. It may be added, finally, that the all-
powerful position of Parliament makes it possible for the
legislature to make any alteration in the present system
which it may wish by simple Act of Parliament. This is not
only the method of passing ordinary legislation in the
United Kingdom, but it is the procedure for effecting any
constitutional amendment whatever.

VII THE POSITION OF THE POLICE FORCES[12]

Although policemen have the duty to enforce the criminal
law, and have wide powers to arrest, they are not servants
of the Crown.[13] The Police Act 1964, however, provides that
a Chief Constable shall be vicariously liable for torts
committed by constables under his direction and control.
All police officers belong to one of the separate and
independent police forces of the country. These are the
county and area police forces, the City of London Police
Force, and the Metropolitan Police Force. Only the last is
truly controlled by the Crown as to matters of policy, etc
for it is under the direct control of the Home Secretary, and
the Crown appoints its Commissioner on the advice of the
Home Secretary. Elsewhere the Home Secretary has the
power to regulate concerning national conditions of service,
which include wage rates, uniforms to be worn, pensions,
etc. The Police Act 1964 also gives him power to call for a
report upon any specific matter from a Chief Constable,
to call upon a local police authority to require a Chief
Constable, or his assistant or deputy, to retire in the

---

12 This section deals only with the position in England and Wales: that for
Scotland and Northern Ireland is somewhat different.
13 *A-G for New South Wales v Perpetual Trustee Co Ltd* [1955] AC 457, [1955]
1 All ER 846.

interests of efficiency, and to cause a local inquiry to be held into the policing of any area. There has been a marked tendency in recent years towards amalgamation of more and more separate forces, which may well lead to increased efficiency and co-operation, and the Home Secretary's powers to instigate amalgamation were increased by the 1964 Act. Each police force is under the control of a police authority which, under the Police and Magistrates' Courts Act 1994, consists of 17 members, nine of whom are drawn from constituent local councils, three from local magistrates and five are independent members appointed by the Home Secretary. Some large areas may be permitted by the Home Secretary to have a police authority with even more members. (The government has recently abandoned the possibility it had considered of creating a police authority for the Metropolitan Police as well.) The Chief Constable in each case is appointed by the relevant police authority. The head of the City of London Police Force is a Commissioner appointed by the Court of Common Council of the City of London Corporation.[14] Nevertheless the Home Secretary maintains certain other indirect control of all the forces, because his approval is necessary for the appointment of any Chief Constable (or Commissioner of the City of London Police) to become effective. The granting of such approval is more than a mere formality, and approval has several times been refused in order to prevent a local man becoming Chief Constable: in the interest of preventing corruption, etc it is thought better that a stranger should be appointed. In addition, any constable or officer who feels himself aggrieved by certain decisions of his local police authority may appeal to the Home Secretary, who has the power to alter such decisions if he sees fit.

Under statutory powers grants are made from the Exchequer to local authorities for various services, including help for financing the local police forces, and it would be possible, though very rare, for any Home Secretary to exert pressure upon a local police authority

---

14   See Chapter 14, below.

by moving to suspend or reduce such payments for particular reasons.[15] Thus the government may maintain some control over the police of the whole country, although full control is limited to the metropolis. The Report of the Royal Commission on the Police, issued in 1962, recommended that more responsibility should be given to the central government to promote coordination between police forces in the work of fighting crime and dealing with traffic, and the 1964 Act has carried out these recommendations. But Dr A. L. Goodhart, in a powerful dissenting memorandum, considered that real efficiency in combating crime could only be achieved by the outright creation of a national force, regionally administered, with the Home Secretary responsible to Parliament for its proper maintenance and administration. It remains to be seen whether Dr Goodhart's more radical views will ever triumph over the trend of cautious evolution which his colleagues on the Royal Commission favoured. At the present time many changes for the structure, conditions of service and control of the police are being considered by the government, but no clear proposals for legislation have yet emerged.

The Police Act 1976 provided for the first time for the establishment of an independent Police Complaints Board which received reports of any investigations by the police of complaints about any members of the police. The Board had the power to direct that disciplinary proceedings should be taken before a Disciplinary Tribunal consisting of the relevant Chief Officer of Police and two members of the Board. This Board was replaced, under the Police and Criminal Evidence Act 1984, by the present Police Complaints Authority which has somewhat stronger powers and greater independence from the police, but some critics of the system for dealing with complaints against the police will not be satisfied until it is completely independent, and no longer involves police officers in the handling of any complaints.

15 Such grants were withheld four times between 1945 and 1964: see B. Whitaker *The Police* (1964) p 91.

VIII THE POSITION OF PUBLIC CORPORATIONS

It is not uncommon for a layman to believe that nationalised industries and monopolies are creatures of the government. This is not necessarily so. Wherever an industry or undertaking has been put upon a national footing, with either a complete or a partial monopoly for one body to exercise, the practice has in the past usually been to create a public corporation by Act of Parliament or by Royal Charter. Instances have been the British Broadcasting Corporation, British Coal, the British Airways Corporation and the British Railways Board, which were incorporated by statute and became legal entities with much the same result as in the case of other companies or corporations. The government very frequently retains the power to nominate or appoint some proportion of the directors or managers of such organisations, and there is no offer of investment facilities for the general public, but they are fully liable (unless the creating statute provides otherwise, which is rare) both criminally and civilly, and they do not normally become servants or agents of the Crown. Their statutes usually provide that reports and accounts are to be submitted to Parliament every year, and in this way Parliament retains some direct control over their affairs, and may decide upon the appropriate sums of money to be voted to them for future operations. But no minister is responsible for the day-to-day running of public corporations, and this means that ministers may not be asked questions about such matters in Parliament.

Since 1979 it has been government policy to transfer or return as many of these corporations to private ownership as possible, and out of the above list only the BBC has so far remained immune to 'privatisation'. Transfers to the private sector in recent years have included British Airways, British Gas and British Steel, the electricity and water industries, and telecommunications. The public sector of industry has shrunk markedly, and in due course there may be only a small residue left.

IX THE ROYAL PREROGATIVE

One last topic remains to be considered in this chapter. The prerogatives of the monarch have always been recognised by the courts in much the same way as they have recognised Parliamentary privilege.[16] Blackstone referred to the royal prerogative as 'that special pre-eminence which the King hath, over and above all other persons, and out of the ordinary course of the Common law, in right of his regal dignity'.[17] But since the Bill of Rights 1689 there is little doubt that such prerogatives as remain to the Crown exist by tacit permission of Parliament. So long as Parliament continues to allow the monarch or the Crown (for most of the prerogatives are now exercised only on the advice of the monarch's ministers) to retain any prerogatives, then those prerogatives will be pre-eminent, but they could always be swept away by Act of Parliament. But since the convention of advice upon which the monarch acts leads to the placing of considerable extra power in the hands of the government of the day, it would appear very unlikely that any government party (or indeed any Opposition party, which in turn hopes to become the government party) should wish to sweep them away. Parliament does, however, occasionally abridge, modify or replace such powers by statute, as, for example, for defence purposes: and one notable instance of a partial abolition of a previously existing prerogative was the passage of the Crown Proceedings Act 1947, which will be discussed in Chapter 12. In a case of 1920,[18] Dicey's definition of the royal prerogative was approved: 'the residue of discretionary or arbitrary authority, which at any given time is legally left in the hands of the Crown.'

It is difficult to find a satisfactory division of the existing prerogatives of the Crown, and it is in any case not intended to give an exhaustive list here, but perhaps the following classification will serve its purpose.

---

16 See Chapter 3, above.
17 I B1 Comm 239.
18 *A-G v De Keyser's Royal Hotel Ltd* [1920] AC 508, [1920] All ER Rep 80.

PREROGATIVES WHICH AFFECT THE PERSON OF THE MONARCH OR
THE STATUS OF THE CROWN

These provide for the monarch's personal immunity from
legal action, that he is not affected by the general law
concerning the disability of infancy, that the Crown is only
to be affected by the passage of a statute if that statute
concerns it expressly or must do so by necessary
implication, and that on the death of one monarch his
successor immediately takes office. The immunity of the
monarch from income tax, which persisted for much of the
twentieth century, was not a result of prerogative but by
virtue of government concession. At the instigation of
Queen Elizabeth II, this immunity was ended in 1993.

PREROGATIVES WHICH ARE OF WIDER IMPLICATION

These may be of an executive, legislative or judicial nature,
and it is convenient to divide them up accordingly.

Legislative

The monarch summons, prorogues and dissolves
Parliament, and he also gives the royal assent to
legislation. He may legislate by Order in Council or by
Proclamation (as explained above) for newly conquered or
ceded colonies, until he has sanctioned a constitution with
a representative legislature in the colony.

The only modern instance of the royal prerogative being
used to dissolve Parliament, and also to dismiss the Prime
Minister and his government without the advice of the
government to do so, was in Australia in 1975. The British
monarch is head of state there, just as in the United
Kingdom, but the prerogative is vested in the Governor-
General, and has nothing to do in reality with the monarch.
It was exercised when the federal government had ceased
to be able to persuade the federal parliament to pass its
measures into law, and had failed either to resign or to call
on the Governor-General to dissolve Parliament with a
view to a general election. Such a use of prerogative power
will clearly be rare, but it illustrates the kind of residuary
power of the monarch which is an important safeguard in
the British Constitution.

Executive

Many of these prerogatives are mere relics of past days, but the more important include the following. The monarch is technically head of all the armed forces. The monarch appoints and dismisses ministers,[19] civil servants, and officers and members of the armed forces. The monarch creates peers and confers honours. The monarch may create corporations by Royal Charter. In cases of national emergency the Crown is responsible for defence of the realm, and is the only judge of the existence of danger from external enemies.[20] The Crown may also, in time of war, requisition ships[1] and enter on private land to repel invasion,[2] although where a statute is applicable it must act under that, rather than under the prerogative power.[3] The requisitioning of ships at very short notice during the Falklands conflict in 1982 was an example of the exercise of such statutory power. In the field of foreign affairs the royal prerogative is perhaps most important of all, for it is within the prerogative to declare war, make peace or enter into treaties, all without recourse to parliamentary approval, although such approval will be required later if the rights of citizens are affected or the expenditure of public money is required. Foreign states, governments or heads of state may be recognised by the Crown, and the sending and receiving of diplomatic representatives is again within the prerogative. A certain defence, known as the defence of 'act of state', may be raised under the prerogative power. It applies in cases where the Crown has done some act in relation to a foreign state or an alien enemy anywhere, or with respect to friendly aliens (ie citizens of foreign countries with which the United Kingdom is not at war) who are outside the monarch's dominions. If such foreign state, alien enemy or friendly alien not within temporary allegiance brings an action

---

19   The monarch, as has been observed above, still appoints the Prime Minister personally, but not the other ministers.
20   *R v Hampden* (1637) 3 State Tr 826.
1   *The Broadmayne* [1916] P 64 at 67.
2   *Case of the King's Prerogative in Saltpetre* (1606) 12 Co Rep 12; *Burmah Oil Co v Lord Advocate* [1965] AC 75, [1964] 2 All ER 348.
3   *A-G v De Keyser's Royal Hotel Ltd* [1920] AC 508, [1920] All ER Rep 80.

against the Crown, the defence of 'act of state' is complete and the action must fail. This is also so where the act was committed by a servant of the Crown under orders, and even where the servant was not under such orders but the Crown has chosen to 'adopt' his act retrospectively.[4] It seems, however, that no 'act of state' defence is available to the Crown in respect of acts committed by the Crown against a British subject anywhere.[5]

Judicial

The monarch is still technically the 'fountain of justice', and the fiction still exists that he is present in *his* own courts, though the judges resolved as long ago as 1607[6] that he may not give an opinion on any case. In theory he normally prosecutes, and all writs are in his name. But it should be remembered that the judges of superior courts no longer hold office at the monarch's pleasure.[7] Again the monarch possesses the prerogative of mercy, in that convicted persons may be pardoned or reprieved by royal command, exercised through the Home Secretary.

From this brief sketch it may be seen that in theory the prerogatives are numerous and wide, but very few of them are still exercised by the monarch in person and according to his own discretion, and all exist only by leave of Parliament. In their present form they are of considerable practical use to any government, and in particular the prerogatives concerning foreign affairs are well-nigh essential for the proper functioning of our relations with other states. It may be that the term 'Royal prerogative' is itself unfortunate in the modern law as it leads some students to believe that the monarch has more real power than is in fact the case. Perhaps 'residuary executive power', or some such expression, might more accurately convey the present position. But the current terminology is a natural result of a monarchical establishment. Provided that it is remembered that 'the Crown' usually

4   *Buron v Denman* (1848) 2 Exch 167.
5   *A-G v Nissan* [1970] AC 179, [1969] 1 All ER 629.
6   *Prohibitions del Roy* (1607) 12 Co Rep 63 at 64.
7   See p 57, above, for the contrary position of Circuit Judges, Recorders and magistrates.

means the whole of the executive, confusion should be eliminated. It is worth noting that the most important part of the monarch's own personal share of the royal prerogative is also its most nebulous area of power, namely the right to advise and warn his ministers, and to be consulted and informed by them.

FURTHER READING

Lord MacDermott *Protection from Power under English Law* (1957) Ch 2
G. Marshall *Police and Government* (1965)
T. C. Hartley and J. A. G. Griffith *Government and Law* (1975)
C. Turpin *British Government and the Constitution, Cases and Materials* (1985)
R. Brazier *Constitutional Practice* (1988).

Chapter 5

The Judiciary

Nothing more than the barest sketch of the system of courts and judges can be attempted in these pages, for the actual identity of the various courts is of little importance in the field of constitutional law. The power of the courts as a whole is what really matters in this respect, and the lawyer is entitled to expect that this power in any given instance will only be wielded by the court having the proper jurisdiction. Should the applicant for any remedy seek it in the wrong court it is the duty of such court to dismiss his application for that reason, and even if the court of first instance should fail to take this step there is always the possibility of appeal to a higher court upon this issue, or else, in the case of what are known as inferior courts, certain extraordinary remedies may be obtained to nullify the first proceedings. It will be noted that we are only concerned specifically with English courts in this chapter. The courts of Scotland and Northern Ireland are quite separate, as will be explained in Chapter 6 below, yet their powers as far as constitutional law is concerned are similar. It is intended in the present chapter, therefore, to consider first the constitutional position of all courts throughout the United Kingdom, and then to outline the nature of the various courts of law in England alone, the doctrine of precedent and the concept of judicial tenure. The English courts will thus be used as exemplifying a *system* which is common in all parts of the United Kingdom.

I THE CONSTITUTIONAL POSITION OF THE COURTS

The primary function of the court is to determine the legality of various kinds of behaviour. This is not to say that it is open to any court to investigate an issue upon its own initiative. In each case it is for an individual to raise the matter as the subject of litigation in which he is involved, whether the issue is one of civil or of criminal law. In the field of criminal law most prosecution in England (the position is rather different in Scotland) is undertaken by the Crown Prosecution Service[1] under the direction of the Director of Public Prosecutions, who is appointed by the Home Secretary. But in some criminal cases and in civil cases of all kinds the litigation may be started by any private individual or by a corporation, as well as by the Crown.

Once an issue has been raised in the appropriate court, it is for that court to reach its decision according to the law of the land. Not infrequently the law is regarded as certain, and the main problem in hand will be to determine the facts in the case before the court and then to apply the law to these particular facts. But sometimes there is doubt about the exact law upon a point, and it is then that the court has a discretion to make its own decision upon the nature of the legal rule involved. As has been seen above in Chapter 2, Parliament in its legislative capacity may, subject only to the primacy of EC law, introduce, alter or repeal any law it thinks fit, and in each case the effect will have been to formulate a new law for the future. Such law is absolutely binding upon all courts,[2] and the only discretion permitted to the courts is that of deciding how the law is to be applied to particular facts. But not all law is statutory. A large part of the law is 'common law', in the sense of having been made by the decisions of courts,

---

1   Set up by the Prosecution of Offences Act 1985.
2   Cf however the possible exception in Scots law, described at p 24, above. Northern Ireland courts are absolutely bound by Acts of the Westminster Parliament, but may declare Acts of the old Northern Ireland Parliament invalid if made outside the powers of that body or in contravention of United Kingdom legislation: see Chapter 6, below.

according to case-precedent where statute law has not yet encroached upon the particular field of law concerned. Although it would be realistic to consider this function as being legislative, yet it is more customary to regard it as adjudicatory upon the various opinions put before the court of what the law on a particular topic may or must be. In either event such decisions may always be overriden by a later Act of Parliament. Perhaps the only way in which it is at all possible for a court effectively to express its opinion upon a statute is by interpretation of the Act when it is arguable that more than one meaning may be accorded to the wording of the Act which is in point. In one or two instances it has been known for courts to interpret statutes in such a way as in effect to flout the intention of Parliament,[3] but such instances are rare, and in any case cannot be blatant, for the bounden duty of the court is to apply the letter of the statute strictly, and in interpreting the meaning of a particular Act its only permitted object is to be able to enforce it once the meaning is discovered.

Until recently the courts had refused to take account of anything said in Parliament during the passage of legislation under interpretation, but the House of Lords ended this self-denying ordinance in 1992.[4] It is now permissible as an aid to statutory interpretation to refer to certain speeches recorded in Hansard (the verbatim record of debates) where (a) the legislation is ambiguous or obscure or the literal meaning leads to an absurdity, and (b) the material clearly discloses the mischief aimed at or the legislative intention lying behind the ambiguous or obscure words of the minister of other promoter of the Bill. The House of Lords considered that such reference would not in any way cut across the parliamentary privilege of freedom of speech in debate enshrined in Article 9 of the Bill of Rights 1689,[5] and they trusted that the Commons would appreciate this.

It will be seen, therefore, that the function of the courts is to discover and apply the law, and so to decide between

3   See the *Anisminic* case, discussed above, p 16.
4   *Pepper v Hart* [1993] AC 593.
5   See above, p 45.

the merits of arguments raised before them by exercising this function. The behaviour of the executive may be scrutinised by the courts upon these principles, and if necessary declared to be illegal, though certain exceptions to this general rule will be discussed later in Chapter 12. But it is never possible for the courts to question the validity of existing Acts of Parliament.[6] In this way the British Constitution differs from that of the majority of other countries of the world. Oddly enough the Constitution of the United States of America also differs upon this point from most other written constitutions, for, although article III vests the federal judicial power in the United States Supreme Court, there is no provision for any power to review legislative Acts of Congress. Yet such a reviewing power has been read into the Constitution by construction, and is now treated as beyond any doubt.[7] Any such Acts which do not conform to the provisions of the Constitution will be held invalid. In the United Kingdom all Acts of Parliament are treated as absolutely binding by the courts, regardless of whether they have any constitutional significance or not,[8] until such time as any particular Act is repealed or altered by Parliament itself in another statute.[9] Thus the courts, like all other institutions of the United Kingdom, have powers subordinate to the one most basic concept of the British Constitution, the sovereignty of Parliament.

II THE ENGLISH COURTS OF LAW

In this brief account it is convenient to divide the English courts into two groups, namely those which have a civil jurisdiction and those with a criminal jurisdiction.

---

6   See, however, footnote 2, p 75. As has been noted already in Chapter 2, no court is bound by any resolution of one of the Houses of Parliament which does not amount to a statute.
7   See particularly the judgment of Chief Justice Marshall in *Marbury v Madison* 1 Cranch 137 (1803); and Learned Hand *The Bill of Rights* (1958) Lecture 1.
8   See Chapter 2, above.
9   Or else by delegated legislation: see Chapter 10, below.

CIVIL COURTS

The lowest courts in the hierarchy are the *magistrates'
courts*, which have a limited jurisdiction over certain types
of small civil disputes. The importance of these courts in
civil cases is now, however, very minor. Most magistrates
are unpaid Justices of the Peace (JPs), appointed and
removable for each area by the Lord Chancellor on the
advice of a local advisory committee (or by the Chancellor
of the Duchy of Lancaster for that county). They are
normally laymen, but they are assisted on points of law
by the clerk of the court wherever they request his help,
provided that he may never advise them on what their
actual decision should be. Since 1966 there has been a short
course of compulsory training for all new JPs. Appeals from
magistrates' courts may be taken to the *Crown Court* or
to a *Divisional Court of the High Court*, both of which
courts will be described presently. If an appeal is taken to
the Crown Court, a further appeal may lie to the Divisional
Court later. Alternatively, the record of a case may be
removed for review by the Divisional Court under the
procedure of certiorari, which will be explained in Chapter
12.

County Courts have existed since 1846, when they were
originally created by the County Courts Act. Their
jurisdiction has been increased in scope several times since
then, and most markedly by the Courts and Legal Services
Act 1990, and now covers all types of minor civil disputes,
with only a few exceptions, and a number of more major
ones. The factor which determines whether a dispute is
minor or major is normally the pecuniary value of the
subject-matter in dispute. Ordinary cases of contract or tort
up to the value of £50,000 in dispute are usually brought
in the County Court, though in other cases concerning, for
example, recovery of land or probate, the limit is higher
or lower according to the statutory provisions in force. The
judges appointed for County Courts are known as Circuit
Judges, and they are appointed and removable by the
monarch on the advice of the Lord Chancellor, and District
Judges appointed by the Lord Chancellor. A jury may sit
if either party wishes it where the sum claimed exceeds
£5, though such a jury is rarely called upon in practice. In

London the County Court retains the name of *Mayor's and City of London Court*. Appeals from decisions of County Courts lie, except in certain rare types of case, to the *Court of Appeal*, which is described below.

All other civil cases are heard in the *High Court of Justice*, which, together with the *Crown Court*, is part of the *Supreme Court of Judicature*, originally created by the Supreme Court of Judicature Act 1873 and now governed by the Courts Act 1971 and the Supreme Court Act 1981. The High Court is divided into the *Chancery Division*, the *Queen's Bench Division* and the *Family Division*, each dealing for the most part with subjects for which it is best suited, although there is no strict rule that a case of any particular kind may only be brought in the appropriate Division and in no other. Generally speaking, however, most property disputes appear in the Chancery Division, the primary business of the Family Division is implicit in its name, and the remainder of civil litigation appears in the Queen's Bench Division. Jury trial is now unusual in civil cases in the High Court, although it is still possible in certain types of dispute. The judges of the High Court are puisne Judges, appointed by the Crown on the advice of the Lord Chancellor. In addition the Lord Chancellor is in strict law the president of the whole High Court and, more particularly, of the Chancery Division, of which latter Division the Master of the Rolls, appointed by the Crown on the advice of the Prime Minister, is another member; but in practice neither will sit in the High Court. The Vice-Chancellor of the Supreme Court is the formal Vice-President of the Chancery Division, and there is a President of the Family Division, while the Lord Chief Justice of England presides over the Queen's Bench Division. These latter judges are appointed by the Crown on the advice of the Prime Minister. For the hearing of cases at first instance the judges sit singly, and it is therefore usual in the High Court (and in the sittings of two or three judges in the Court of Appeal, discussed below) to find several judges sitting in different 'courts' at the same time, each exercising the full power of the court. But for certain special purposes, such as the hearing of appeals from magistrates' courts, the judges of the High Court may

sit in benches of two or three as a *Divisional Court* of one
or other of the Divisions, normally of the Queen's Bench
Division. The High Court usually sits in London, but it may
also sit in other parts of the country.

Appeals from the High Court or the County Court lie to
the *Civil Division of the Court of Appeal*, the judges of
which are the Master of the Rolls and the Lords Justices
of Appeal, appointed by the Crown on the advice of the
Prime Minister. They normally sit as a bench of two or
three. The Lord Chancellor, the Lord Chief Justice, the
President of the Family Division, the Vice-Chancellor and
the Lords of Appeal in Ordinary are also members of the
court, but in practice the president is the Master of the
Rolls and only the Lords Justices normally sit with him.

The ultimate court of Appeal in civil cases from English,
Scottish or Northern Ireland courts is the *House of Lords*,
where the judges are the Lords of Appeal in Ordinary ('Law
Lords'), appointed by the Crown on the advice of the Prime
Minister, who must have a quorum of three, but frequently
sit as a group of five, and occasionally even of seven.[10] Lay
peers may not, by convention, sit when the House is
hearing appeals, but any peers who hold or have held high
judicial office may sit. The president is the Lord
Chancellor. The House normally hears appeals in a
committee room, and not in the legislative chamber. In
certain special cases appeals in civil proceedings may go
direct from the High Court to the House of Lords.

One modification of this entirely municipal system of
courts is provided by certain articles of the treaties
establishing the European Community, which, since the
European Communities Act 1972, now bind the whole of
the United Kingdom.[11] Where any question regarding the
interpretation of the European treaties, or regarding the
interpretation or validity of the acts of the institutions of
the Communities, is raised before a court or tribunal of any
member state, that court or tribunal may request the
European Court of Justice to give a ruling thereon before

10   As they did in *Pepper v Hart*, see above p 76, fn 4.
11   See Chapter 2, above.

proceeding further with the case in hand. And such a reference to the European Court must be made if there is no further judicial remedy against the ultimate decision of the court or tribunal concerned. Accordingly there will be some circumstances in which the House of Lords, and any other court or tribunal which is of last resort, will be bound first to refer questions to the European Court. The judges of the Court of Justice are drawn from the member states, there being at least one from each state, but some of its work is now done in its own Court of First Instance with separate judges.

At this stage the *Judicial Committee of the Privy Council* should also be mentioned, as it is the ultimate court of appeal from the courts of the Isle of Man, the Channel Islands, the various colonies and dependencies of the United Kingdom, and from the courts of such of the independent members of the Commonwealth as have not abolished the right of appeal to it. The Committee also hears certain appeals from special tribunals, such as the General Medical Council, and gives advice to Parliament upon legal matters which may occasionally be referred to it.[12] The composition of the Board, as it is called, is often the same as for the hearing of appeals in the House of Lords, although Privy Councillors who are not Lords of Appeal are sometimes admitted to membership in view of their judicial experience in other Commonwealth countries. In recent years the membership of the Judicial Committee has been widened, and more Commonwealth judges have been appointed as Privy Councillors so that they might sit for the hearing of appeals. As has been pointed out in Chapter 4, all Lords of Appeal are Privy Councillors. The decisions of the Board are strictly speaking in the form of advice to the Crown, and only one 'judgement' used to be given by the whole Board, but since 1966 it has been permissible for members to deliver dissenting opinions.

---

12 See, eg, *Re Parliamentary Privilege Act 1770* [1958] AC 331, [1958] 2 All ER 329.

CRIMINAL COURTS[13]

As before, the *magistrates' courts* are lowest in the hierarchy of courts, but they are of far more importance for the trial of persons charged with criminal offences than in civil proceedings, since they are responsible for the trial summarily of more than 95% of all accused persons. Such trial is of the persons accused of what may be generally described as the less serious offences. Because of the preponderance of this type of crime, particularly in large urban areas, stipendiary magistrates are sometimes appointed to relieve or take the place of JPs, and metropolitan stipendiary magistrates sit in the London boroughs. Specially qualified magistrates sit in *Juvenile Courts* with special powers. Although normally JPs sit as a bench of at least two, a stipendiary or metropolitan stipendiary magistrate may sit alone and has the same powers as any two JPs. Appeals from magistrates' courts in criminal cases lie, as in civil cases, to the *Crown Court* and the *Divisional Court of the Queen's Bench Division*.

The trial of all criminal offences of the graver variety is always before a jury, and held in the *Crown Court*. These courts, created by the Courts Act 1971, are held in various centres throughout the country, and they are presided over by High Court Judges, Circuit Judges or Recorders, the latter being barristers or solicitors appointed to act in this judicial capacity on a part-time basis. There is also provision for JPs to sit with a judge when the Crown Court is hearing appeals from the decisions of magistrates' courts. The Crown Court in London retains the name of its predecessor, the *Central Criminal Court*. Appeal from any conviction before a Crown Court lies, at the instance of the defendant only, to the *Criminal Division of the Court of Appeal*, which in any sitting consists normally of two (or occasionally three) judges, one of whom is usually a Lord Justice of Appeal and the other either the Lord Chief Justice or a puisne Judge of the Queen's Bench Division.

---

13   It is not proposed to discuss the *coroners' courts* here, as they do not actually have the function of trying a case to reach a decision upon any particular person's guilt.

The *Courts-Martial Appeal Court,* composed in the same way as the criminal division of the Court of Appeal, and first set up by statute in 1951, hears appeals from conviction by courts-martial, but it is not necessary here to consider the disciplinary powers of courts within the armed forces. The Royal Commission on Criminal Justice, which reported in 1993, has made a number of recommendations designed to speed up and improve criminal trials by, eg, restricting some rights to jury trial, but it remains to be seen how far these will be implemented.

Once more the final court of appeal is the *House of Lords.* An appeal lies, at the instance of either the defendant or the prosecutor, from a decision of the criminal division of the Court of Appeal, the Courts-Martial Appeal Court or the Divisional Court, wherever the court below certifies that a point of law of general public importance is involved and it appears either to that court or to the House of Lords that the point is one which ought to be considered by the House.[14] But, in distinction from its civil jurisdiction, the House has no power to hear a criminal appeal from Scotland. The *Judicial Committee of the Privy Council* may hear criminal appeals from jurisdictions outside the United Kingdom, but only where it appears that there may have been grave mismanagement or a serious miscarriage of justice.

III THE DOCTRINE OF PRECEDENT

The doctrine of stare decisis, which has been built up in England, and which is mirrored in Scotland and Northern Ireland, provides that decisions of the *House of Lords* are binding upon all lower courts and also usually upon itself. But in 1966 the Lord Chancellor, with the agreement of all the Law Lords, stated that the House of Lords would in future consider itself able to depart from any previous decision of the House when it appears right to do so.

14 Administration of Justice Act 1960 and Criminal Appeal Act 1968.

Subject to the overriding jurisdiction of the Lords, decisions of the *Courts of Appeal* and of the *Divisional Court* are normally binding upon themselves and upon lower courts, but the qualifications upon this statement are too technical to explain in this book.[15] Decisions of the *High Court* or *Crown Court* are probably binding on inferior courts, but they are only highly persuasive upon later sittings of their own courts. All the courts that have been mentioned are regarded as 'superior courts', except for the magistrates' courts and County Courts, which are 'inferior courts'. Decisions of inferior courts do not bind other inferior courts, and they cannot be regarded as highly persuasive. Any persuasive value which they possess at all is likely to be short-lived, as cases before these courts are not reported in any recognised series of reports.

The precedent value of any court decision is, of course, always subject to alteration by Act of Parliament.

IV JUDICIAL TENURE

Judges of inferior courts may be removed from office by the Lord Chancellor (though this is a rare occurrence), but Circuit Judges may only be so removed on the grounds of incapacity or misbehaviour.[16] It is of particular importance, however, that all judges of superior courts (that is, High Court Judges and above) have a much greater safeguard to their tenure of office. Although they must retire at the age of 70,[17] they may in practice only be removed before that age by the Crown after an address requesting such removal by both Houses of Parliament. This provision was first enacted in the Act of Settlement 1700, and the relevant statutes in force today are the Supreme Court Act

---

15 See *Young v Bristol Aeroplane Co Ltd*[1944] KB 718, [1944] 2 All ER 293.
16 The only modern instance of such removal in England was in December 1983 when a Circuit Judge who had been convicted of customs offences was dismissed for misconduct. In 1992 a Sheriff (who holds a somewhat similar office in the Scots court system) was removed.
17 The Judicial Pensions and Retirement Act 1993 imposes this age limit for all holders of judicial office appointed after the Act is in force.

1981 and the Appellate Jurisdiction Act 1876 (concerning Lords of Appeal in Ordinary).[18] Although it is sometimes alleged that it is undesirable that the judiciary should depend for their continued tenure of office upon the goodwill of the legislature, it is significant that over a period of nearly 300 years no English judges have ever been so removed. In addition the salary of all judges is charged on the Consolidated Fund, and is not reviewed each year by the House of Commons with the other estimates of national expenditure.

There is, however, a possible restriction upon the tenure of the higher judiciary which was introduced by the Supreme Court Act 1981. If the Lord Chancellor is satisfied, by means of a medical certificate, that any judge of the Supreme Court is disabled by a permanent infirmity from performing his judicial duties, and is for the time being incapacitated from resigning his office, he may declare that judge's office to have been vacated. In the case of the Lord Chief Justice, the Master of the Rolls, the President of the Family Division or the Vice-Chancellor, the declaration requires the concurrence of two of their number; in the case of a Lord Justice of Appeal it requires the concurrence of the Master of the Rolls; and in the case of a puisne Judge of any Division of the High Court it requires the concurrence of the senior judge of that Division. Although no judge's office has yet been declared vacant under this procedure, it is surely reasonable to have this power available in the event of, eg, a judge being rendered paralysed and speechless by a stroke. This modification of the principle of judicial independence established by the Act of Settlement 1700 is thus no significant infringement of judicial tenure.

FURTHER READING

H. G. Hanbury and D. C. M. Yardley *English Courts of Law* (5th edn, by D. C. M. Yardley 1979)

---

18 A possible reserve power to dismiss, vested in the Crown alone, is discussed in, eg, Hood Phillips, *Constitutional and Administrative Law* (7th edn, 1987) p 387.

G. R. Y. Radcliffe and Lord Cross of Chelsea *The English Legal System* (6th edn, by G. J. Hand and D. J. Bentley, 1977)

A. K. R. Kiralfy *The English Legal System* (8th edn, 1990)

O. Hood Phillips and A. H. Hudson *A First Book of English Law* (8th edn, 1988)

R. M. Jackson *The Machinery of Justice in England* (7th edn, 1977)

R. J. Walker and M. G. Walker *The English Legal System* (6th edn, 1985)

K. J. Eddey *The English Legal System* (5th edn, 1992)

P. F. Smith and S. H. Bailey *The Modern English Legal System* (2nd edn, 1991).

Chapter 6

Scotland, Wales, Northern Ireland, the Isle of Man and the Channel Islands

In the present chapter it is intended briefly to sketch the importance so far as British constitutional law is concerned of those other parts of the British Isles which are not automatically subject to the municipal law of England. The relationships between each of these countries have already been mentioned in Chapter 1.

I SCOTLAND AND WALES

The separate Kingdoms of England and Scotland became associated by the personal union of the Crowns of both countries when James VI of Scotland succeeded to the throne of England as King James I in 1603, but the complete unification of the two countries in a political sense did not occur until the Treaty of Union, which was ratified by Acts of the two Parliaments of England and Scotland in 1707. The effect of the Treaty and Acts was to abolish the two Parliaments and to form a new Parliament of Great Britain, and thus ultimately a government of the whole country, in Westminster. This position has been altered by the later union with Ireland, discussed below, only to the extent of increasing the jurisdiction of Parliament to cover the whole of the newly formed United Kingdom, and the full legislative authority of Parliament over both countries remains.[1] It has, however, remained customary to appoint six or seven members of each government to

---

1   With the possible exception exemplified in the case of *MacCormick v Lord Advocate* 1953 SC 396, discussed in Chapter 2, above.

special responsibility over Scottish affairs, and in particular there is always a Secretary of State for Scotland.

The Scottish courts of law, legal professions and legal systems have not been affected by the union, except in so far as Parliamentary authority was transferred to Westminster, and that the House of Lords became the ultimate court of appeal, though only in civil cases, as has been seen above in Chapter 5. The legal systems of England and Scotland have had widely different histories and traditions, but it is not our present purpose to examine them. The superior Scottish civil courts are the Inner and Outer Houses of the Court of Session, of which the Inner House, which sits in two Divisions, presided over by the Lord President and the Lord Justice-Clerk respectively, exercises appellate jurisdiction, while ten Lords of Session sit singly in the Outer House, as Lords Ordinary, to hear cases at first instance. The superior criminal court is the High Court of Justiciary, consisting of the same judges as the Court of Session but under the titles of Lord Justice-General, Lord Justice-Clerk and Lords Commissioners of Justiciary, which exercises both trial jurisdiction (one Lord with a jury) in Edinburgh or on circuit, and appellate jurisdiction. The inferior courts in criminal cases are the district courts, and in civil matters the Sheriff Courts, presided over by Sheriffs. Appeals lie in civil cases either to the Sheriff Principal and then on to the Inner House of the Court of Session, or directly to the Inner House of the Court of Session, and in criminal cases to the High Court of Justiciary. The Scottish equivalent of the English Attorney-General is the Lord Advocate, though he does not occupy the position of head of the Scottish Bar.

In recent years there has been a movement in favour of some devolution of legislative and executive power from Westminster to Scotland and Wales. The Report of the Royal Commission on the Constitution, published in 1973,[2] recommended the establishment of separate Scottish and Welsh Assemblies, though the Commissioners were unable to agree on many of the details of their proposals. The recommendations were in any case highly contentious and

2   Cmnd 5460.

politically charged, but the Labour Government which held office from 1974 to 1979, after first publishing a White Paper detailing its intentions, introduced a Scotland and Wales Bill into Parliament. The main purpose of the Bill was to establish an Assembly and an Executive in Scotland, which should have legislative and executive powers over a fairly wide range of topics, and a smaller Assembly in Wales, with only executive powers and over a rather more limited range of topics. Powers of veto were to be retained by the Secretaries of State for Scotland and Wales respectively, and the whole of the power to tax should remain at Westminster. The Bill attracted opposition in the House of Commons not only from the Conservative Opposition but also from a number of Labour dissidents and some of the smaller parties, and it had to be abandoned after the government was defeated on a timetable motion in February 1977.

Towards the end of the same year the government then introduced two Bills designed to achieve devolution of some power to the two provinces separately, and this time it was successful in steering them through Parliament. The Scotland Act 1978 and the Wales Act 1978 duly received the royal assent, but each Act provided that it should only come into operation on such day as the Secretary of State should by order appoint, and that any such order required the approval by resolution of both Houses of Parliament. But no draft of such an order was to be laid before Parliament until a referendum had been held in the province concerned. A referendum was then held in Scotland and in Wales in March 1979, when the question asked was: 'Do you want the provisions of the Scotland (or Wales) Act 1978, to be put into effect?' If it appeared to the Secretary of State, having regard to the answers in the referendum and all other circumstances, that the Act should not be brought into effect, he was then empowered to lay before Parliament a draft Order-in-Council providing for its repeal, and this draft would require to be approved by Parliament in the same way as an order to bring the Act into force. In the event the results of the referenda showed a majority in favour of the proposed devolution in Scotland which was insufficient to justify bringing the provisions of the Scotland Act into force, and a 4-1 majority against such devolution in Wales. Accordingly one of the first acts of the Conservative Government which came to power after the General Election of May 1979 was to obtain the approval of Parliament for the repeal of the two Acts by Order-in-Council. Nevertheless it remains a possibility that some further scheme for devolution of power to Scotland or Wales may emerge at a future date.

II NORTHERN IRELAND

Northern Ireland is a part of the United Kingdom of Great Britain and Northern Ireland, as has already been seen in Chapter 1. Its law, like that of England and Wales, is a common law system, in that it is derived partly from parliamentary statutes and partly from case law decided in the courts of the land. Prior to the Union with Ireland Act 1800, the Parliament of Ireland had legislative authority over the whole of Ireland, although some authority was at times claimed by the Parliament of England (up till 1707) and by the Parliament of Great Britain (between 1707 and 1800), for Ireland held the status of a lesser Kingdom under the English, and later the British, Crown. Between 1800 and 1922 only the Parliament of the United Kingdom of Great Britain and Ireland had this authority; and after the Irish Free State (Agreement) Act 1922, which followed the partition of Northern and Southern Ireland (the latter having since become the Republic of Ireland, and separate from the British Crown), the legislative power over Northern Ireland was held partly by the United Kingdom Parliament in Westminster and partly by the Northern Ireland Parliament at Stormont.

The Constitution of Northern Ireland, as laid down in the Government of Ireland Act 1920, involving the partition of Ireland and the creation of the Stormont Parliament, was always a matter of contention and gave rise from time to time to extremist action of a violent nature. As a result of a particularly serious wave of disorder and terrorism starting in 1969, the British

Parliament prorogued the Stormont Parliament by the Northern Ireland (Temporary Provisions) Act 1972, and imposed direct rule over the province from Westminster, such rule being exercised by a new Secretary of State for Northern Ireland. The government made it clear at the time that it was intended as soon as possible to make further provisions for devolution of power to the province, and such provisions were made in the Northern Ireland Assembly Act 1973, and the Northern Ireland Constitution Act 1973, which also includes a charter of human rights for the province. In view of the fact that the Unionist Party had been in the majority in Stormont continuously from 1922 to 1972, and that no other party had been able to take part in the formation of the Northern Ireland Executive, it was provided that elections to the new Assembly were to be by a type of proportional representation, so that the proportion of members of the various political parties in the Assembly would largely mirror the number of votes cast for the parties at the preceding election for the Assembly. The Executive also, when formed, was to consist of members of both the majority and minority groups. The Act did not stipulate how the mixed Executive was to be set up, but appointments were to be made by the Secretary of State for Northern Ireland, who was to be satisfied that the Executive was likely to be widely accepted throughout the community.

Unfortunately both the Assembly and the new Executive proved to be unworkable because the different political parties refused to work with each other. The Assembly, although elected only in 1973, was therefore dissolved, along with the Executive, less than a year later by the Northern Ireland Act 1974. The 1974 Act also made provision for a Constitutional Convention, which was elected in 1975. Its function was to work out a means of forming a power-sharing administration for Northern Ireland. But again the new body failed, this time because the United Ulster Unionists, who had an overall majority of members of the Convention, refused to make any recommendation for power-sharing with other parties. Eventually the Convention was dissolved in 1976, and direct rule over the province from Westminster reimposed.

The latest attempt to devolve power to Northern Ireland is the Northern Ireland Act 1982, which makes arrangements for what has been called 'rolling devolution'. Under the Act there is provision for election to a new Northern Ireland Assembly, which will at first possess only scrutinising, deliberative and consultative functions. The first election to this Assembly took place in October 1982 by the single transferable voting system. The Assembly was asked to recommend to the Secretary of State arrangements under which the whole or part of the range of legislative and executive responsibilities previously transferred by the 1973 legislation could be exercised by the Assembly and by a devolved administration answerable to it. Thereafter, provided certain criteria were satisfied, the government would recommend to Parliament that the arrangements so recommended should be implemented and appropriate powers transferred. Yet again, however, the arrangements foundered on the rock of inter-party intransigence in the province, and the Assembly was dissolved in 1986, though the provisions of the 1982 Act remain law so that it is still possible for fresh elections for the Assembly to take place in the future.

Meanwhile in 1985 an Agreement was entered into between the governments of the United Kingdom and the Republic of Ireland, under which the Republic is accorded some limited part to play in fashioning future developments for the province. The Agreement recognises the present status of Northern Ireland as part of the United Kingdom, and declares that legislation to create a united Ireland will only be introduced into both Parliaments if and when a majority of the people of Northern Ireland clearly desire this and formally consent to it. More particularly the Agreement provides for cross-border co-operation on a number of practical matters, including political, security and legal issues, and for the holding of formal conferences between the two governments at various levels. Predictably this so-called Anglo-Irish Agreement has been controversial, and it is not yet clear whether it will in the long run be any more successful than the other efforts made in this century to settle the constitutional and other problems of Northern Ireland, but an application made to the High Court in London by the Leader of the Ulster Unionist Party at Westminster for a declaration that it was contrary to law failed on the grounds that the Agreement was akin to an international treaty made within the Royal prerogative, and that it did not conflict with any existing Act of Parliament.[3]

It has to be conceded that at the time of writing there is no very clear way forward for a permanent settlement of Northern Ireland. Legislation to provide special powers for the police and security forces in their efforts to keep the peace has been required, and the latest measure is the Northern Ireland (Emergency Provisions) Act 1991, which needs annual renewal and in any case expires after five years. The population of the United Kingdom is about 58 millions, of whom over 48 millions live in England, 5 millions in Scotland, some 2.9 millions in Wales and 1.5 millions in Northern Ireland. It would seem logical to imagine that a reasonable solution to the constitutional and other problems of Northern Ireland could be found, and successive British governments have certainly tried hard to do this during the past 30 years. The present world climate of nationalism and fragmentation may not help, but it can be expected that the efforts will continue, especially since a glimmer of hope has been provided by the terrorist ceasefire in the autumn of 1994.

All the above developments had left untouched the arrangements whereby 12 MPs were elected in Northern Ireland constituencies for the House of Commons at Westminster, where they possess equal powers and status with members elected from other parts of the Kingdom. But the House of Commons (Redistribution of Seats) Act 1979 made provision for the number of Northern Ireland seats in the Commons to be increased to between 16 and 18, the exact number to be settled after a report from the Northern Ireland Boundary Commission. The eventual result was to increase the number of seats to 17.

The law of Northern Ireland, although strictly an entirely separate system from that of England, is in practice very like it, partly because of the long history of close

3   *Molyneaux , ex p* [1986] 1 WLR 331.

association, and later actual union, with the mother country, and partly because its legal development today tends to mirror that of its British partner. The courts of Northern Ireland are very like those of England. Thus there is a Supreme Court of Judicature of Northern Ireland, consisting of a Crown Court, a High Court and a Court of Appeal, the latter of which sits in Belfast. Further appeals from the Court of Appeal in civil cases, and in criminal cases under similar conditions to those which exist in England, lie to the House of Lords at Westminster, which in such cases must act as the highest court of appeal for purposes of Northern Ireland law. The officers and judges of the Northern Ireland courts bear similar titles to those of their English counterparts.

III THE ISLE OF MAN

The Isle of Man is a separate dependency of the British Crown, and is not part of the United Kingdom, although Acts of the United Kingdom Parliament will apply to the island provided they do so expressly or by necessary implication. The legislature, one of the oldest in the world, is called the Court of Tynwald, and it is composed of the Lieutenant-Governor, the Legislative Council and the House of Keys. Until 1980 the Lieutenant-Governor presided over the Legislative Council, the other members being the Bishop of Sodor and Man, the First Deemster, the Attorney-General, and seven members elected by the House of Keys. However the Legislative Council now has its own separate elected president, and the other former ex officio members of the Council have since been excluded from it. The House of Keys consists of 24 elected members, and there must be a fresh election at least every five years. The Tynwald is responsible for most internal legislation, which must receive the royal assent, but certain important subjects, such as air navigation and merchant shipping, are usually dealt with by the United Kingdom Parliament.

The executive authority is vested in the Lieutenant-Governor, who is responsible, among other things, for defence, but in recent years he has been assisted by an

Executive Council, over which he has, since 1980, ceased to preside. The royal assent to legislation of the Tynwald is normally signified through the Lieutenant-Governor.

The law of the island, known as 'breast law', is quite distinct from English law, though it tends more and more to resemble the latter today. The courts of the island are also distinct, and the judges are called Deemsters. The most important courts are the Staff of Government, which deals with civil cases, and the Court of Criminal Appeal, from either of which a further appeal lies to the Judicial Committee of the Privy Council.

IV THE CHANNEL ISLANDS

The Channel Islands may in a sense claim to have been older dependencies of the English Crown than any other parts of the present British Isles, for they belonged to the Dukes of Normandy before England was annexed to the Duchy. The two main islands are Jersey and Guernsey, Alderney and Sark being dependencies of the latter. Although the islanders in theory deny the right of the United Kingdom Parliament to legislate for them, in practice they do not dispute it, and United Kingdom legislation is frequently extended to the islands by Order in Council. The laws of the islands are of Norman origin, and are distinct from those of England. A word or two should be said about each island.

JERSEY

The local legislature is the States of Jersey, consisting of the Bailiff, who is nominated by the Crown and who presides, the Attorney-General, Solicitor-General, the Dean of Jersey, 12 senators, who are elected for 9 years, 12 constables or mayors of the parishes and 28 deputies, who are elected for three years. The royal assent is necessary before any legislation may come into force. The Lieutenant-Governor and certain island officials hold executive authority, and the Royal Court, presided over by the Bailiff or Deputy Bailiff, hears both civil and criminal cases, there being an appeal to the Court of Appeal for the Channel Islands, and a further appeal to the Privy Council in civil cases and also, with special leave of the Privy Council, in criminal cases where there may have been a grave miscarriage of justice.

GUERNSEY

The institutions of the Bailiwick of Guernsey are mainly similar to those of Jersey. The State, however, consists of the Bailiff, Attorney-General, Solicitor-General, 12 conseillers, 33 elected People's Deputies and 12 elected douzeniers. *Alderney,* although a dependency, maintains its own legislature, consisting of a President and nine members, all elected. *Sark,* another dependency, remains a feudal seignory, under the titular control of the hereditary Seigneur or Dame of Sark. Its legislature is the Chief Pleas, consisting of the Seigneur, the Seneschal, who is appointed by the Seigneur with the approval of the Lieutenant-Governor of Guernsey, 12 elected deputies and the 40 tenement holders.

FURTHER READING

G. W. Keeton and D. Lloyd, with specialist contributors *The United Kingdom, the Development of its Laws and Constitutions: Part I. England and Wales, Northern Ireland and the Isle of Man* (1955)

T. B. Smith and L. A. Sheridan *The United Kingdom, the Development of its Laws and Constitutions: Part II. Scotland and the Channel Islands* (1955) (replaced, so far as Scotland only is concerned, by Professor Smith's later book: see below)

T. B. Smith *Scotland: The Development of its Laws and Constitution* (1962) (also published in Scotland as *A Short Commentary on the Law of Scotland*)

H. Calvert *Constitutional Law in Northern Ireland* (1968)

D. M. Walker *The Scottish Legal System* (5th edn, 1981).

Chapter 7

Rights and Duties of the Citizen

In many written constitutions the fundamental rights of the citizen are specifically set out in the constitutional document, as in the first eight and the fourteenth amendments to the Constitution of the United States of America, or, to take a more modern example, in the earlier articles of the Constitution of India, which came into force in January 1950. But of course this is not the case as regards the inhabitants of the United Kingdom, for we have no such constitutional document. It would, however, be unrealistic to consider that the citizens of a democratic state should possess no guarantees safeguarding their individual liberties, for such could only result from a recognition that the state was itself of a totalitarian rather than a democratic nature. Similarly it would be unrealistic to consider that the same citizens were under no corresponding duties to their fellow citizens and to the nation as a whole. Nevertheless it is as well to remember that such individual rights and duties as do exist in the United Kingdom are always subject to the overall power of alteration or abolition by Act of Parliament, for, as we have already seen in Chapter 2, the most basic of all constitutional factors in the United Kingdom is the almost unrestricted legislative power of Parliament.

In recent years there has been some pressure of a political nature for the enactment of formal statutory civil rights for the United Kingdom. It is not without interest that in the Northern Ireland Constitution Act 1973 there is for the first time a charter of human rights for the province, and that in particular it lays down that any legislation or executive action which is discriminatory on political or religious grounds is unlawful. Perhaps this could be a forerunner of similar legislation for the United Kingdom as a whole, or at least for any action taken in Scotland or Wales if power is ever devolved to those countries from Westminster. It is, however, of note that the Standing Advisory Commission on Human Rights reported in 1977[1] that, although it favoured the incorporation of the European Convention on Human Rights 1950 into the domestic law of the United Kingdom as a whole, it could see no advantage in enacting more comprehensive civil liberties provisions for Northern Ireland alone. Such legislation of itself can neither cure violence nor create a consensus upon which to base a further effort at devolved government for the province.

It is unlikely that a written document of civil liberties would do anything more to protect fundamental rights in the United Kingdom than is already achieved, but it might be of general educative value, and it could also provide a useful guide for legislators in their everyday work. It might well also enable some litigants to gain redress in British courts instead of needing to seek it in The European Court of Human Rights, as discussed above in Chapter 2. It seems a very remote possibility that Parliament should ever in the foreseeable future embark upon the enactment of a written constitution for the United Kingdom, but of course if this should ever happen the constitution would need to cover the subject of civil liberties specifically.

I THE RULE OF LAW

Few phrases in recent years have become so well known by all members of the community as 'the rule of law', and yet it is doubtful whether many of the people who commonly use the expression have more than a very vague idea what they mean by it. It is used most frequently by politicians and statesmen who essay to decry the actions of other political parties or foreign governments on the

1   'The Protection of Human Rights by Law in Northern Ireland', Cmnd 7009.

ground that they do not measure up to the standards of common decency and fair dealing which they themselves believe they stand for. This use of the term is not incorrect, for it is not a technical expression, but it is certainly not a use which stems from any exact knowledge of its meaning; and as lawyers it is important that we should be able to define as far as possible the type of fair dealing to be regarded as the standard behaviour within the meaning of the expression. The most logical attempt in the sphere of international affairs that has been made to discover and explain the meaning of the phrase has been by the International Commission of Jurists, an independent international organisation, not set up by the United Nations but enjoying consultative status with the United Nations Economic and Social Council. The purpose of the International Commission is to draw the attention of all governments and peoples to any actions by any country or government anywhere in the world which have the effect of curtailing the basic liberties of any members of the community.

The activities of statesmen, and even of lawyers, in the international sphere are not, however, of any immediate significance in municipal British constitutional law. Yet the rule of law is still of some importance within that municipal law, and it is therefore our duty to investigate its nature and function. In doing so we must to some extent anticipate the contents of Part II of this book, for many developments in English administrative law have provided useful illustrations of the working of the rule of law. But it is best to leave consideration of the scope and details of administrative law until the basic principles of constitutional law have been explained. Many jurists through the centuries have been interested in the concept of the rule of law, but any modern discussion of the subject must begin with the theory of Professor A. V. Dicey, first published in 1885 in his *Introduction to the Study of the Law of the Constitution*, because discussion of the concept in this country has for the past century centred round his ideas about the expression. Dicey divided the rule of law into three parts, explained by the following extracts:

(1) '. . . no man is punishable or can be lawfully made to suffer in body or goods except for a distinct breach of law established in the ordinary legal manner before the ordinary courts of the land. In this sense the rule of law is contrasted with every system of government based on the exercise by persons in authority of wide, arbitrary, or discretionary powers of constraint . . . It means, in the first place, the absolute supremacy or predominance of regular law as opposed to the influence of arbitrary power, and excludes the existence of arbitrariness, of prerogative or even a wide discretionary authority on the part of the government';[2]

(2) '. . . every man, whatever be his rank or condition, is subject to the ordinary law of the realm and amenable to the jurisdiction of the ordinary tribunals';[3]

(3) '. . . the general principles of the constitution (as for example the right to personal liberty or the right of public meeting) are with us the result of judicial decisions determining the rights of private persons in particular cases brought before the courts; whereas under many foreign constitutions the security (such as it is) given to the rights of individuals results, or appears to result, from the general principles of the constitution . . . Our constitution, in short, is a judge-made constitution. . .'[4]

It can be seen that the first two parts of the rule are closely allied, and may be said to amount to the concept of equality before the law for all citizens. The maxim *nullum crimen sine lege* would be apposite here. It may be noted that the arbitrary rule of the Nazi government in Germany and elsewhere in the 1930s and 1940s, with the accompanying activities of the Gestapo, was in clear breach of the first part of Dicey's rule, as were also the totalitarian acts of many Communist governments after the Second World War. Dicey did in fact go on to contrast English law with that of France, in which country there existed (as there still

2   Op cit (10th edn, 1959) pp 188, 202.
3   Op cit, p 193.
4   Op cit, pp 195, 196.

exists today) a separate system of administrative courts, which had jurisdiction over all disputes between the state and individuals, to the exclusion of the ordinary courts of law. Many critics of Dicey have believed that he was asserting that no such thing as administrative law existed in this country, but such criticism has been unjust, for he intended to say no more than that we had no separate *droit administratif* with its own special courts. As was clear to him and to all English lawyers, there must always be a branch of law amounting to administrative law, because no country can survive without an administration, and any such administration must possess certain legal rights, powers and duties which impinge in some way upon the lives and rights of the ordinary citizens of the land. Dicey did in fact publish a paper in the Law Quarterly Review in 1915 entitled 'The Development of Administrative Law in England',[5] and it is now clear that he only intended to declare that in this country the ordinary courts had jurisdiction over questions of administrative law, just as over all branches of the law, whatever the rules of those branches may be. Where he was wrong was in believing that the French system favoured the state to the detriment of the rights of the ordinary citizens of France, and that thus the existence of the administrative courts was in conflict with the rule of law. If one accepts Dicey's distinction between the two systems as correct, with the exception of his mistaken distrust of the French administrative courts, and that the ordinary courts deal with English administrative law problems, then there is one way at least in which the laws of the United Kingdom may have progressed away from the concept of the rule of law since the time of his writing, for, as we shall see in Chapter 11, a large number of administrative tribunals have been created since his time, and these tribunals have jurisdiction over much litigation of all kinds in the field of administrative law. Their existence may be strictly contrary to Dicey's first branch of the rule, but at least none of them ought to favour the executive to the derogation of the rights of individuals, and all are subject to control by

5   31 LQR 148.

the ordinary courts of the land, as will be explained in Chapter 12.

It is not hard to find a number of other examples in our laws which must be exceptions to the first two branches of Dicey's concept. Foreign sovereigns and diplomats enjoy special immunity from criminal prosecution or civil action, and judges can never be held civilly liable for anything done or said in the course of their office. Members of both Houses of Parliament enjoy extensive privileges, which have already been discussed in Chapter 3, while peers are disqualified from voting in parliamentary elections. Trades Unions occupy a special privileged position in that they cannot normally be rendered liable in tort at all,[6] although this legal immunity was only conferred for the first time by the Trade Disputes Act 1906, some 20 years after Dicey first published his theory, and it has been much reduced by provisions in the Trade Union and Labour Relations Act 1974 and the Employment Act 1982. Police powers of arrest without warrant may be regarded as infringements upon individual liberty, even though they are unlikely to be used in an entirely arbitrary manner in this country, as we shall see presently. Discretionary powers may always be conferred upon the executive, or indeed upon anyone, by Act of Parliament, the most usual example being the power to make delegated legislation,[7] and powers of a somewhat similar nature may be conferred also by the royal prerogative. But at the time of Dicey's writing probably the most glaring exception from his rule was the immunity from the ordinary process of law which had been accorded to the Crown as a result of the royal prerogative, an immunity in which Parliament had acquiesced, for it could be useful to the government or to any future government. As we shall see in Chapter 12, this exception has been largely eliminated by the passage of the Crown Proceedings Act 1947 and it is now true to say that in one very important respect our law has approached more

---

6   For a powerful condemnation of this present Trade Union immunity, see Lord MacDermott *Protection from Powers under English Law* (1957) Ch 7.

7   See Chapter 10, below.

nearly to the concept of the rule of law which Dicey had propounded.

It would be impossible to iron out all the inequalities. Perhaps the clearest example of all inequalities which are essential in civilised communities is provided by the age of criminal responsibility. It is unthinkable that a new-born baby or a very young child should bear full criminal responsibility for his activities. So the rule of law, even for Dicey, cannot have meant equal *treatment* for all before the law. It is enough that the same law covers us all, even though it makes different provisions for different groups of people — and it is of course always possible for the ordinary citizen to join a Trade Union or to become an MP. Yet the fact that the various exceptions within the law may be recognised by the law in a totalitarian state is not enough to satisfy the principle of the rule of law. As the International Commission of Jurists has repeatedly stressed, a legal system must also provide for a proper balance, with judicial safeguards, between the interests of the state and of individuals, an independent judiciary and Bar, and social institutions allowing for the dignity of man.

The third branch of Dicey's rule is largely true, provided it is accepted that the concept of the sovereignty of Parliament is based on the decisions of the courts to that effect. Certainly it is true that the constitution is part of the ordinary law of the land, and is not contained in any special instrument or instruments. The sovereignty of Parliament has been discussed already in Chapter 2, and we need not elaborate upon it further here, but its very existence renders the first two branches of Dicey's rule subject to a possible enormous practical exception.

The great value of Dicey's work in this field has been to provide lawyers and jurists with an ideal. It is not possible to formulate a satisfactory definition of the rule of law, and indeed it cannot seriously be contended that any one 'rule' as such has any place in the law of the United Kingdom, which depends primarily on the rules laid down by Parliament and secondarily upon the concrete decisions of the courts. If such a theoretical 'rule' has no place among the detailed statutes and decisions from which our law is drawn, then it cannot be considered as a basic tenet of our constitutional law. But as a guide to law-makers and reformers it can be of inestimable value, and for this purpose it is of little importance whether one accepts the views of Dicey or of any other jurists, or constructs an entirely new idea concerning its identity. Providing the aim is the preservation of the liberty and rights of all members of the community, and that only such exceptions from this aim are allowed as are essential to the administration of the nation in an orderly fashion (such as judicial and parliamentary privilege, with proper safeguards), the purpose of the rule of law will have been fulfilled. In short, the rule of law is not a rule or a law, but a persuasive guide for the legislature, the executive and the judiciary, linked in practice, in the United Kingdom, with the working of many of the conventions which mitigate the theoretical deficiencies in the constitution, and mould it into a living democratic entity.

II RIGHTS OF THE CITIZEN IN THE UNITED KINGDOM

The declaration of rights of the citizen in the modern sense really dates from the latter part of the eighteenth century, when the revolutions in America and France took place. The theorists and politicians of both these countries borrowed their ideas from the writings of Locke, who, after the Bloodless Revolution of 1688–1689, wrote about natural rights in his *Two Treaties of Civil Government*. Blackstone in the mid-eighteenth century had also lectured and written on the subject of the individual's fundamental rights,[8] and his influence was greatly felt upon the laws and the Constitution of the United States.[9] The American Declaration of Independence in 1776 and the so-called 'Bill of Rights' (the constitutional amendments mentioned above[10]) in 1791 provided inter alia for the preservation of

8   *Commentaries on the Laws of England* Vol 1.
9   See H. G. Hanbury *The Vinerian Chair and Legal Education* (1958) Ch III.
10 The first eight amendments apply to federal rights, and the fourteenth amendment applies to the states.

such fundamental rights as freedom of religion, speech, the press, peaceful assembly, and that there should be no deprivation of life, liberty or property without due process of law. The French Declaration of the Rights of Man in 1789 covers very much similar ground, and a far more recent example of such an instrument is provided by the Universal Declaration of Human Rights, adopted by the United Nations General Assembly in 1948, although it may well be felt that the statesmen of some of the countries which supported the latter Declaration did so with their tongues in their cheeks, and certain International Covenants on Human Rights adopted by the General Assembly in 1966. It should be noted that the Universal Declaration of Human Rights has no legal force in any country unless expressly adopted in its municipal law. The same may be said of the European Convention for the Protection of Human Rights and Fundamental Freedoms, drawn up in 1950, though most Western European countries, including the United Kingdom, which subscribed to the Convention, undertook thereby certain basic obligations and agreed to set up, where necessary, machinery for the investigation of an adjudication concerning the civil liberties with which the Convention dealt. The acceptance by the United Kingdom government of the competence of the European Court of Human Rights has already been mentioned in Chapter 2. Its practical effect is that any United Kingdom citizen who has exhausted his domestic legal remedies may apply to the Court for a remedy against the violation of any of the fundamental rights set out in the European Convention.

In England it is only possible to select certain statutes or charters as having the most significance constitutionally. These purport to perform somewhat similar functions, and include Magna Carta 1215, the Petition of Right 1627, and the Bill of Rights 1689, all having appeared before the time of Locke's writings. None of these documents is really a statute in our modern sense, for they only amount to the acceptance by the monarch of certain demands by Parliament or his people. But they have always been treated as of statutory force. The latter two documents were mainly concerned with the freedom of

Parliament in the face of the power of the monarch rather than with the individual liberties of each citizen, and Magna Carta primarily protected the privileges of the barons, but it is the spirit of English law to discover general principles from particular instances.[11] Although there is no need in the present work to examine the documents closely, many basic freedoms have been deduced from them and also from the representative character of Parliament, which, it is argued, would not be permitted by the electorate to exercise such extreme legislative authority unless it did so primarily as a means of protecting and safeguarding the lawful interests and freedoms of the populace. It is therefore assumed that basically all citizens are free to do and act as they please, and that this liberty will only be curtailed in so far as limitation may be essential for the due and just administration of the whole country, and then only by law and not by arbitrary power. The stability of British institutions, strengthened by the good fortune of centuries of steady growth, unhampered by foreign invasion, is enough to render otiose any more codified list of civil liberties. Even though some prerogative powers cut across individual liberty, they only exist so long as Parliament permits them to remain in the interests of the community, as has already been pointed out in Chapter 4. Thus, as far as British constitutional law is concerned, our main task is to determine in what ways individual liberty is *restricted* by law, and not how it is preserved. We shall also, however, consider the remedies provided by law for the infringement of such fundamental rights as citizens do possess. Our approach must be primarily negative, but for convenience we may assume that certain basic rights exist except where they have been curtailed by the law, whether statute or common law, and these rights may be said to be:

(1)   freedom of the person to behave as he pleases;
(2)   equality before the law;
(3)   freedom of property;

11   See Roscoe Pound *The Development of Constitutional Guarantees of Liberty* (1957) Chs 1 and 2.

(4)   the right to free elections;
(5)   freedom of speech and to write;
(6)   freedom of public worship;
(7)   freedom of assembly and association; and
(8)   family rights.

It is possible that to this list may be added the right to work and the right to withhold one's labour.

Some limitations upon the foregoing list are obvious and need not be further explained. Thus freedom of speech and writing must of necessity be restricted by the law of defamation, which in itself is protecting other individuals, and by such laws as those of sedition, censorship, contempt of court, obscenity, and the prevention of disclosure of matters concerning national security. Freedom of property is subject to the levying of taxes, without which the administration of the country would collapse, and to statutory powers of compulsory acquisition. Again, equality before the law is a rule with several important exceptions. As has been seen, judges and MPs must receive special protection from ordinary legal process so that they may carry out their duties efficiently, and the same largely applies to diplomats; whereas infants under the age of majority cannot be held fully responsible in law for all their actions.

But other exceptions to the basic freedoms require some explanation. The detailed limitations discussed in this chapter are rules of English law only, unless otherwise indicated, but the laws of Northern Ireland and Scotland are not very dissimilar.

Incursions upon freedom of the person and property

Every man is free to do as he wishes unless the law otherwise provides, as, for example, by the law of assault, or by the law making it an offence to drive a motor vehicle having consumed alcohol in such a quantity that the proportion in the blood, as ascertained by a compulsory laboratory test, exceeds the prescribed limit.[12] A different statutory limitation was found in s 3 of the Trade Disputes Act 1906, where it was provided that an act done by a person in contemplation of furtherance of a trade dispute should not be actionable on the sole ground that it may interfere with the right of some other person to dispose of his capital or his labour as he wills. Thus, by implication, an individual could find his power to dispose of capital or labour hampered without being able to take action to re-establish his right so to dispose of it, unless the person interfering with his right had also offended against the law in some other respect, such as by being guilty of a conspiracy in furtherance of private vengeance.[13] He would also have been powerless to redress the wrong if the additional offence amounted to a tort and it was committed by a Trade Union or Unions, or by Union members in contemplation or furtherance of a trade dispute, as was also provided by the Act of 1906. Later legislation has, however, restricted the effect of the 1906 Act to acts necessarily connected with the particular industrial dispute, and so such acts as the picketing of other workplaces are no longer protected.

Any arrest of a person must normally be with the authority of a warrant signed by a magistrate and executed by a police officer; and such a warrant will only be issued where the magistrate is satisfied that the grounds for the warrant are lawful. Warrants must name the individual to be arrested specifically, for it was held in 1765[14] that 'general warrants' were illegal. In that case a warrant for the arrest of the authors, printers and publishers of 'The North Briton' was held to be too general. One of the most celebrated of all English constitutional law cases is *Entick v Carrington*, decided in the same year,[15] in which the plaintiff, who was suspected of being the author of 'The Monitor, or British Freeholder', obtained £300 damages for trespass committed by Carrington and certain other King's

---

12   A provision first introduced by the Road Safety Act 1967, Pt 1, and much strengthened by later legislation.
13   See, eg, *Huntley v Thornton* [1957] 1 All ER 234, [1957] 1 WLR 321.
14   *Money v Leach* (1765) 3 Burr 1742.
15   (1765) 19 State Tr 1029.

messengers, who had broken and entered his house and seized his papers and books under a general search warrant issued by a Secretary of State. In petty cases accused persons are 'summoned', and a warrant will only issue if the summons is disobeyed. Arrest without warrant by a police officer is permitted, inter alia, where he has a reasonable suspicion that a person has committed an arrestable offence, which is defined by the Police and Criminal Evidence Act 1984 as any offence for which the sentence is fixed by law (ie murder and treason), offences carrying a penalty of five years' or more imprisonment, and various other offences listed in the Act. Any other citizen may without a warrant arrest a person who is in the act of committing such a crime, or where such crime has actually been committed, or if he is called upon to assist a constable or magistrate. There are also certain other special statutory provisions for arrest without warrant, and these have been rationalised by the 1984 Act. Any person arrested without a warrant must be told, either in technical or non-technical language, the true ground of arrest. It is not sufficient merely to state the general ground, such as 'murder', unless the circumstances are obvious, as when the accused has been caught in the act of committing an offence. In a House of Lords case in 1947[16] two police officers were held liable for false imprisonment after wrongfully arresting the plaintiff without a warrant and misinforming him as to the actual charge to be brought against him.

Because of the incidence of modern terrorism, especially by the IRA, special powers of arrest and detention of suspected terrorists are contained in the Northern Ireland (Emergency Provisions) Act 1991. The intention is that these powers shall cease once terrorism has been sufficiently curtailed.

POLICE POWERS OF SEARCH AND ENTRY

Although the normal rule is that no person may enter private premises without permission from the owner or

16   *Christie v Leachinsky* [1947] AC 573, [1947] 1 All ER 567.

occupant, police may, under the provisions of the Police and Criminal Evidence Act 1984, enter and search any premises in order to execute a warrant of arrest, to arrest a person for an arrestable offence or certain other specified offences, to recapture a person unlawfully at large, to save life or limb or prevent serious damage to property. Except in the last event, however, there must be reasonable grounds for believing the person sought is on the premises. Under s 78 of the 1984 Act, moreover, it is provided that the court may refuse to admit evidence where, having regard to all the circumstances, including those in which the evidence was obtained, the admission of the evidence would have such an adverse effect on the fairness of the proceedings that the court ought not to admit it. This latter provision effectively replaces the earlier and widely criticised common law rule established in the case of *Elias v Pasmore*[17] in 1934 that where police lawfully enter private premises to arrest a man, but do not possess a search warrant, they will still be excused if they take documents or search the premises, provided that they discover something which is useful as evidence in the prosecution of the arrested person, or even of some other person altogether. This could amount to a dangerous accretion of power in the hands of the police, even though it was made clear in the case itself that the accused would still have a right of civil action against the police for trespass, etc in respect of any documents searched or taken away which proved to be of no use for a prosecution. The replacement of the old common law rule is to be welcomed. It stemmed from the economically and politically troubled times of the 1930s, when considerable difficulty was experienced in controlling the public meetings and activities of Communists and Fascists. But a clear statutory basis for police powers of search and entry is more satisfactory, even though it still gives a court discretion to admit evidence obtained by, eg, undercover operations.

Concerning a more general run of criminal activity it is of note that the Theft Act 1968, s 25(3), provides that a

17   [1934] 2 KB 164, 103 LJKB 223.

person who is authorised to search premises for stolen goods may seize any goods he believes to be stolen, and that such seizure is legal whether or not the goods turn out in the end to have been stolen. There are also powers under the Police and Criminal Evidence Act 1984 and the Criminal Justice Act 1988 to search persons who have been lawfully detained.

When a police officer is lawfully on premises he has wide powers to seize articles found there, whether or not they relate to offences for which the owner or occupier has been arrested, but the officer must have reasonable grounds for believing that they were obtained in consequence of the commission of an offence or else that they amount to evidence in relation to any offence. It is, however, necessary also that the officer believes seizure to be necessary to prevent the items concerned being concealed, lost, altered, destroyed or damaged. Although the dilemma concerning how far police may be permitted to go in searching for evidence of crime, and to what extent evidence obtained by irregular methods may be used in court, has thus now been faced by Parliament, it may be doubted whether all controversy has yet been stilled.

A further possibility of invasion of private premises by the police without warrant is instanced by the case of *Thomas v Sawkins*,[18] which provides a limitation at common law upon the general right to hold a public meeting on private property. There it was held that the police may enter private premises without a warrant if they have reasonable grounds to believe that, if they are not present, seditious speeches will be made or breaches of the peace will take place. It appears, therefore, that a general licence to the public to enter private premises may be revoked as concerns anyone except a policeman, who may in his discretion override such a revocation. Such a police power is, however, limited, for it has also been held[19] that a power of entry without warrant does not exist where the commission or future commission of merely a summary offence has been suspected.

18 [1935] 2 KB 249, 104 LJKB 572, one of the few common law rules in this area left untouched by the Police and Criminal Evidence Act 1984.
19 *Davis v Lisle* [1936] 2 KB 434, [1936] 2 All ER 213.

Certain statutory powers of entry and search have also been conferred upon civil servants, public corporation officers, inspectors of gas and electricity meters, health visitors, etc; and powers of entry, inspection of documents and detention of property are given by such recent legislation as the Finance Act 1987, Banking Act 1987, Fire Safety and Safety of Places of Sport Act 1987, and the Crossbows Act 1987.

POSTAL INTERCEPTION AND TELEPHONE TAPPING

The interception of letters and particularly of telephone conversations has quite often been used as an aid to the maintenance of law and order. There have often been fears that the use of such a weapon could amount to a dangerous incursion upon normal civil liberties, but a Committee of Privy Councillors reported in 1957 that the opening of mail and tapping of telephones in certain circumstances for the defence of the realm was within the royal prerogative. Nevertheless in 1984 the European Court of Human Rights held that such telephone tapping was a violation of human rights. As a result Parliament passed the Interception of Communications Act 1985, under which it is an offence to intercept a communication by post or by a public telecommunications system unless the Home Secretary has (under certain conditions and safeguards) issued a warrant requiring the addressee to intercept specified communications. A person who believes his communications have been illegally intercepted may apply to an independent tribunal established by the Act which has wide powers to report to the Prime Minister, quash warrants improperly granted, direct the destruction of documents, and order the Secretary of State to pay compensation. The Security Service Act 1989 provides that complaints about surveillance by members of the security service may also be considered by an independent tribunal; and a committee of both Houses of Parliament has been set up to oversee all the security services, under the terms of the Intelligence Services Act 1994.

EMERGENCY POWERS AND MARTIAL LAW

Statutory emergency powers provide a further great infringement of personal and property freedoms. There is no need to consider them in detail here, for each such power is conferred for a particular purpose at a particular time, especially in war-time. The powers are thus of many different kinds and depend entirely upon the need which Parliament and the government deem has asserted itself at the time. They supplement, and in many ways supplant, such prerogative powers as exist to restrict individual liberty in times of stress.[20]

Martial law means the suspension of ordinary law, and the substitution therefor of discretionary government by the executive, exercised by the military. It is thought to be among the royal prerogatives to be able to proclaim martial law, though only in times of war. Such a power has not been exercised in England since the time of Charles I, and it is arguable that the prerogative has been superseded by parliamentary supremacy. Certainly it is most unlikely that the Crown should attempt to declare martial law, as Emergency Powers Acts are probably more efficacious. The Crown has, however, sometimes set up military tribunals under its prerogative power when a state of war existed, as for instance in Ireland in the early 1920s.[1] It is also conceivable that the parliamentary procedure might become impossible to work in the event of, say, a nuclear attack upon London without warning, but it might be more realistic to consider such a situation not as one where the prerogative power came into its own, but as one where whoever was left alive would take upon himself the task of trying to restore some order out of the wreckage.

REMEDIES FOR WRONGFUL DEPRIVATION OF LIBERTY OR PROPERTY

Where there has been wrongful invasion of a person's liberty or property he may have any of the following remedies:

---

20 See Chapter 4, above; eg, *Case of the King's Prerogative in Saltpetre* (1606) 12 Co Rep 12.
1 See, eg, *Re Clifford & O'Sullivan* [1921] 2 AC 570.

(1)   a civil action for damages, such as for assault, false imprisonment, malicious prosecution, trespass to the person, land or goods, etc;

(2)   a similar action for recovery of property;

(3)   a criminal prosecution for assault, battery or theft, etc;

(4)   a writ of habeas corpus to obtain his release from custody;

(5)   perhaps a prerogative order to quash a proceeding wrongly taken against him;

(6)   an appeal to a higher court, if the encroachment upon his liberty or property has been by court process; or occasionally

(7)   the right to take out a summons before a magistrate to recover costs of defending irregular and unjustifiable proceedings.

Of these remedies, the prerogative orders will be discussed in Chapter 12, and only habeas corpus requires any further explanation here.

HABEAS CORPUS

The prerogative writ of habeas corpus ad subjiciendum has for many centuries been one of the most important safeguards of individual liberty, and is still regarded as the ultimate weapon of defence for the oppressed.[2] The exact machinery and effect of the writ has been reformed by statute from time to time in order to ensure its full efficiency, the most notable of such statutes being the Habeas Corpus Acts of 1679 and 1816. An applicant for the writ must allege that he or the complainant is being unlawfully detained, whether it be for a criminal or civil offence, or for no offence at all (as, for example, where it is alleged that A is being prevented from leaving his own house by B). Frequently the application is made through an interested friend or relative of the imprisoned person. A prima facie case must be made out before the writ will issue, but if a superior court or judge grants the issue of

2   It may perhaps be noted here that the right to habeas corpus has been suspended in Northern Ireland, where the executive has had certain powers of discretionary imprisonment, since 1939.

the writ the effect is to cause the alleged captor to 'bring the body' of the prisoner before the judge, who will then decide on the merits of the case whether there is any legal ground for continuing to detain him. If no such legal ground is found to exist the applicant is set free by the court. Until 1960, for example, it was not uncommon for persons detained in mental institutions to apply for the writ, and such applications were not infrequently successful because magistrates had exceeded their powers.[3]

If an application for the writ had been turned down, no second application will be entertained by any court in any circumstances on the same grounds unless fresh evidence is adduced. This rule was introduced by the Administration of Justice Act 1960 to resolve certain doubts which had persisted up to that time. In the same Act the opportunity was taken to widen the rules concerning appeals, which had previously only been possible in civil cases. Although no appeal is permitted from the order of a single judge granting an application for habeas corpus in a criminal case, appeals *are* now permitted from any decisions of the Divisional Court, whether to grant or to disallow applications for the writ, and they lie, as in other criminal cases, direct to the House of Lords. But such appeals are not hampered by the necessity for the Divisional Court to certify that a case involves a point of law of general public importance which applies in other criminal appeals,[4] and so it is probably easier to appeal in a habeas corpus case than in any other criminal case. It is also provided that, although a single judge may grant an application for the writ, only the Divisional Court may refuse it, so that any single judge to whom an application has been made, and who is disposed to disallow it, must refer the application to the full Divisional Court.

---

3   Under the provisions of the Mental Health Act 1959 these powers of magistrates were in effect surrendered to the medical profession. Two doctors, one of whom must have special psychiatric qualifications, are empowered to order a patient's compulsory detention in hospital for a period of either 28 days or up to a year in the first instance. The patient has a right of appeal from such an order to a Mental Health Review Tribunal.

4   See Chapter 5, above.

Incursions upon freedom of assembly and association

Although the practice of meeting or demonstrating peacefully in public is common and not in itself unlawful, there are a number of criminal offences which reduce the general freedom of assembly and association. Originally developed by the common law, most of these offences have now been replaced by newly-defined crimes created by the Public Order Act 1986. The offences to be considered in this section are as follows.

CONSPIRACY

A combination or agreement of two or more persons to do an unlawful act, or to do a lawful act by unlawful means, is an indictable offence. Thus any assembly or association which amounts to a conspiracy will be criminal. Such assemblies must, however, be distinguished from the activities of Trades Unions, which are legal associations with the principal object of collective bargaining about wages and conditions of work.[5]

AFFRAY

A person is guilty of an affray if he uses or threatens unlawful violence towards another and his conduct is such as would cause a person of reasonable firmness present at the scene to fear for his personal safety.

RIOT

This offence is committed where twelve or more persons present together use or threaten unlawful violence for a common purpose, and their conduct is such as would cause a person of reasonable firmness present at the scene to fear for his personal safety.

---

5   Trade Union Act 1871; Trade Union and Labour Relations Act 1974.

VIOLENT DISORDER

This is committed in the same way as riot, except that only three or more persons need be involved, and there is no requirement of a common purpose. The offence has been employed in combating violence at or near football matches.

UNLAWFUL VIOLENCE

Causing fear of, or provoking the immediate use of, unlawful violence by threatening, abusive or insulting words or behaviour, or the distribution or display of writings or signs to another which are threatening, abusive or insulting, amounts to the offence of unlawful violence.

MISCELLANEOUS STATUTORY OFFENCES

It may be noted that the above crimes are usually committed in public places, and on this score they may be compared with police powers in respect of private premises, such as are exemplified in *Thomas v Sawkins*,[6] discussed above. Various Acts of Parliament establish other offences, such as unlawful drilling, seditious meetings, tumultuous petitioning, carrying an offensive weapon at a public meeting or in a procession, and wearing in any public place or at any public meeting a uniform signifying association with any political organisation or with the promotion of any political object. Only two such offences need be mentioned specially here, namely the offence first laid down by s 5 of the Public Order Act 1936, strengthened by the Race Relations Act 1976, s 70, and finally replaced by the Public Order Act 1986, ss 17-19, as incitement to racial hatred; and that of obstruction or assault of the police, now governed by the Police Act 1964, s 51.

Any person in a public place or at a public meeting who uses threatening, abusive or insulting words, or indulges in suchlike behaviour, or distributes or displays any writing, sign or visible representation of like effect, and who intends to stir up racial hatred, or if racial hatred is

6   [1935] 2 KB 249, 104 LJKB 572.

likely to be stirred up thereby, is guilty of the offence now provided by the Public Order Act 1986. Provisions designed further to eliminate other aspects of racial discrimination and persistent harassment are to be found in the Race Relations Act 1976, replacing earlier Acts of 1965 and 1968, and the Criminal Justice and Public Order Act 1994. Similar legislative provisions make sex discrimination unlawful in almost all circumstances, the most recent measure being the Employment Act 1989.

Any person who wilfully obstructs a police officer in the course of his duty may be arrested without warrant. It is clear that this is a case where a policeman who has a suspicion that an unlawful assembly might take place can avoid having to wait and see, and can simply order the persons concerned to disperse. Any disobedience would then amount to obstruction.[7] But a decision in 1966 emphasises that obstruction of a police officer is not unlawful unless it is also wilful.[8] The appellant had been seen by a police officer acting suspiciously late at night in a district where a number of breaking offences had been committed on the same night. On being questioned, he refused to give his full name and address, to say where he was going or where he had come from, or to accompany the officer to a police box in order that his identity might be established. The Divisional Court held that he was entitled to refuse to do all these things until he had been arrested, that 'wilful' imported something done without lawful excuse, and that no obstruction without lawful excuse had been established in this case. Accordingly they quashed his conviction. Again it has been held that obstruction of a police officer is not in itself unlawful, giving rise to the right of the officer to effect an arrest without a warrant, unless the officer is actually acting in the execution of his duty.[9] And an assault upon a police officer in the execution of his duty is only committed, within the terms of the Police Act 1964, s 51, if the officer actually *was* executing his duty. Thus there is a good defence to such a charge if physical

7   As happened in *Duncan v Jones* [1936] 1 KB 218, 105 LJKB 71.
8   *Rice v Connolly* [1966] 2 QB 414, [1966] 2 All ER 649.
9   *Wershof v Metropolitan Police Comr* [1978] 3 All ER 540.

resistance is put up against police officers who are attempting to detain and search a person unlawfully.[10]

Once more the powers of the police are prominent as being the agency whereby the legal limitations are enforced. It will be noticed that, as before, much is left to the discretion of the individual police officer, and it may be argued that such exercise of discretion could be subjective. Police officers might be able to order law-abiding people to move away from a department store or a busy street for no apparent reason. Police are also much concerned with preventing and remedying traffic obstruction, and in enforcing local by-laws,[11] in both of which occupations they are empowered to exercise a wide discretion. Again, an officer might arrest without a warrant because he believed the individual arrested had committed an offence or was about to do so, or he might enter private property where he believed a person who had committed an arrestable offence was there, whereas no other reasonable policeman would have drawn the same conclusion, and it might be argued that such an arrest or entry would nevertheless be lawful. This solution would be undesirable, and although the point has not been decided directly it is probably correct to consider that belief in the commission or likely commission of an offence must be reasonable in the objective sense. Thus the policeman must behave as a 'reasonable policeman'.[12] If this principle is accepted there is little danger that the extensive police power in this field of the law will ever be seriously abused.

10 *R v Waterfield* [1964] 1 QB 164, [1963] 3 All ER 659.
11 These are explained in Chapters 10 and 14, below.
12 Lord Hewart CJ, in *Thomas v Sawkins* [1935] 2 KB 249 at 254, [1935] All ER Rep 655 at 657, above, said: 'I think that there is quite sufficient ground for the proposition that it is part of the preventive power and, therefore, part of the preventive duty, of the police, in cases where there are such reasonable grounds of apprehension as the justices found here, to enter and remain on private premises . . .' See also *Piddington v Bates* [1960] 3 All ER 660, [1961] 1 WLR 162 (an appeal to the Divisional Court from conviction for obstruction of police officers in execution of their duty); and *Broome v DPP* [1974] 1 All ER 314 (a Trade Union picket who had blocked the path of a lorry about to enter a 'blacked' building site, having failed to dissuade its driver from proceeding, and who also disobeyed a police order to move, was found guilty of obstructing the highway).

Offences against the state

Any commission of a criminal offence amounts to an abuse of the limits of personal freedom permitted by the law, as also, in a different way, does the commission of any tort. It is not intended in this section to consider all criminal offences, but only those crimes against the state which are of such fundamental importance as to occupy a place in our constitutional law. Only three groups of these offences, treason, sedition, and offences against the Official Secrets Acts, need be discussed specially.

TREASON

The most important statute concerning treason is the Statute of Treason 1351, which is generally regarded as having been declaratory of the common law at the time, and which is still in force, although amended and added to in comparatively minor ways by subsequent Acts, primarily by statutes passed in 1702, 1707, 1795 and 1817. Under the Statute of Treason the following types of conduct amount to the offence:

(1)   compassing the death of the King, the Queen or their eldest son and heir. An overt Act is, however, necessary to prove the commission of this offence;

(2)   violating the King's consort, or eldest unmarried daughter, or his eldest son's wife;

(3)   levying war against the King in his realm;

(4)   adhering to the King's enemies in the realm, giving them aid and comfort in the realm or outside. It has been held that the offence is committed whether the adherence is within or without the realm;[13]

(5)   slaying the Chancellor, Treasurer or the King's Justices, while in the discharge of their offices.

---

13   *R v Lynch* [1903] 1 KB 444, 72 LJKB 167, where a British subject became a naturalised subject of the Boer Republic during the Boer War, and fought against the British. See also *R v Casement* [1917] 1 KB 98, 86 LJKB 467, where another British subject, during the 1914-18 War, incited British prisoners of war in Germany to join the enemy forces and take part in an expedition against the British in Ireland; and *Joyce v DPP* [1946] AC 347, [1946] 1 All ER 186, discussed below.

Two further types of treason added by later statutes are:

(6) attempting to hinder the succession to the throne of any person entitled to succeed under the Act of Settlement 1700;
(7) maintaining in writing the invalidity of the line of succession established by the Act of Settlement.

Treason is punishable by death,[14] and any prosecution for treason must be initiated within three years of the commission of the offence.

SEDITION

A seditious intention is an intention to bring into hatred or contempt, or to excite disaffection against, the monarch in person, or the government and constitution of the United Kingdom as established by law, or either House of Parliament or the administration of justice, or to excite subjects of the Crown to attempt, otherwise than by lawful means, the alteration of any matter in Church or state by law established, or to raise discontent or disaffection among subjects of the Crown, or to promote feelings of ill-will and hostility between different classes of such subjects. So runs the description given of it by Cave J in 1886.[15] Prosecutions for sedition are now rare, and are not normally instituted unless incitement to violence has taken place, but the term 'sedition' may cover any of three common law offences:

(1) publication of a seditious libel, that is, publication in a permanent form of matter of a seditious nature;
(2) uttering of seditious words;
(3) conspiring to do an act in furtherance of a seditious intention.

OFFENCES AGAINST THE OFFICIAL SECRETS ACTS

Because the treasons listed as (3) and (4) above under TREASON can only really be committed in war-time (the

---

14 This is now the only criminal offence in the United Kingdom for which the capital penalty remains.
15 *R v Burns* (1886) 16 Cox CC 355.

definition of an 'enemy' being a citizen of a country with which the United Kingdom is at war), it has been found necessary to legislate with respect to offences of spying and sabotage[16] in peacetime. The Official Secrets Acts 1911 and 1920 made it an offence, inter alia:

(1)   for any purpose prejudicial to the safety or interests of the state to approach, inspect or enter any prohibited place, ie an army or air force establishment, naval ship, arsenal, etc;

(2)   to make sketches or plans which might be useful to an enemy;

(3)   carelessly to part with such documents, or to retain them longer than permitted;

(4)   to communicate documents or information to any person which might be useful to an enemy;

(5)   to obstruct any of Her Majesty's forces in the vicinity of any prohibited place; or

(6)   to wear an unauthorised uniform, to make a false declaration or to forge a passport or permit in order to gain admission to a prohibited place.

The width of the provisions in (3) and (4) above was often criticised, and in 1972 a Department Committee headed by Lord Franks recommended some modification of the law intended to ensure that prosecutions should be confined to cases where the alleged acts of the accused concern matters of real importance.

Eventually the Official Secrets Act 1989 accomplished much of what had been recommended, and now it is no longer a criminal offence to disclose information unless it harms national security or concerns certain other sensitive matters, though it remains an offence for those connected with the security services to disclose details about their work. The 1989 Act also provides that anyone charged with an offence of disclosure has a defence if he does not know, or has no reasonable cause to believe, that the information falls within the statutory prohibition, or that its disclosure

---

16   The use of prosecutions under the Official Secrets Acts in order to deal with acts of sabotage as well as spying was made clear by the House of Lords in *Chandler v DPP* [1964] AC 763, [1962] 3 All ER 142.

would be damaging. English law is still far from providing the sort of general freedom of information existing in many other countries, but this may come before too long.

MISCELLANEOUS OFFENCES

A number of other offences against the state should be borne in mind as of constitutional importance, but no attempt will be made here to explain or discuss them. The majority of them are statutory offences, and the list includes misprision of treason (concealment of the offence of treason), attempts to alarm or injure the monarch, incitement to mutiny or disaffection, trading with the enemy, and offences against the Foreign Enlistment Act 1870.

ALLEGIANCE

In the case of treason and many of its kindred offences it is necessary before any prosecution can succeed that it should be proved that the accused owes allegiance to the Crown. The categories of persons who owe such allegiance are:

(1) British citizens;
(2) British dependent territories citizens, British overseas citizens and aliens resident in the United Kingdom; and
(3) British dependent territories citizens, British overseas citizens and aliens not resident in the United Kingdom, but who have previously been so resident, and have left either their families or their effects in the United Kingdom.

A short explanation of these three groups of persons is necessary.

British citizens

Until 1983 the attributes of British nationality were governed by many statutes, the most important of which was the British Nationality Act 1948. But a wholesale reform was effected by the British Nationality Act 1981, which came into force in 1983, and which fundamentally altered the basis upon which British citizenship is acquired. This ended some seven centuries of legal tradition under which birth in the kingdom gave an automatic right to citizenship, and replaced it with rules based much more on the continental system of citizenship by descent. Full British citizenship is thus now restricted to those with close personal connections with the United Kingdom, the Channel Islands and the Isle of Man. A child born in the United Kingdom will be a British citizen if the father or mother is a British citizen or is settled in the kingdom in the sense of being entitled to stay indefinitely. In addition there are detailed provisions concerning the acquisition of citizenship by descent, if a child is born abroad, by registration and by naturalisation. British citizens have full rights of entry into the United Kingdom and residence there.

The 1981 Act creates two other categories of citizen: (i) British dependent territories citizens, who are those living in the remaining British colonies, and who thereby have the right to enter and live in their own territories, but not in the United Kingdom; and (ii) British overseas citizens, who are those who were British subjects and citizens of the United Kingdom and colonies under the 1948 Act, but who have not become British citizens or British dependent territories citizens under the 1981 Act. British overseas citizenship carries no special rights.

Other Commonwealth countries have their own citizenship rules. Commonwealth countries for this purpose are the independent member states of the Commonwealth, together with certain other countries which may not yet be fully independent, though independent in many respects, and which have been granted by the United Kingdom the privilege of possessing their own citizenship. It may be that a prime significance of this innovation in constitutional law is that, as far as the laws of the United Kingdom are concerned, only British citizens are now capable of committing treason by an act outside the United Kingdom and colonies, though there is as yet no case authority for this assertion. It is submitted that it is more accurate today to consider that for the purpose of the law of treason only British citizens owe permanent allegiance to the Crown.

British dependent territories citizens, British overseas citizens and aliens who owe temporary allegiance

In view of what has just been said, citizens of other Commonwealth countries may be regarded as coming into the same category as British dependent territories citizens, British overseas citizens and aliens for the purposes of allegiance to the criminal laws of the United Kingdom, though not for all other purposes. The citizens of the Republic of Ireland, which is not a country within the Commonwealth at all, possess certain privileges under the terms of the Ireland Act 1949, and they are not for other purposes regarded as aliens, but again they come into the same category as aliens as far as the law of treason is concerned. Bearing this in mind, no explanation of the description 'aliens resident in the United Kingdom' is required here. But non-resident aliens under group (3) above need some attention. The authority for the existence of the group is a resolution of the English judges in 1707[17] to the effect that any alien who had once resided in Great Britain,[18] and who had then departed from the country, but leaving his family or estate behind him, could still be dealt with as a traitor if he should transgress the law of treason — provided he returned or was brought back within the jurisdiction of the courts, for the trial of an absent man for treason would be abortive. The meaning of this resolution seems plain, but it has probably been rather broadened in scope as a result of the case of *Joyce v Director of Public Prosecutions* in 1946.[19] In that case William Joyce, nicknamed 'Lord Haw-Haw' in the United Kingdom, was tried and convicted for treason on the ground that he had broadcast for and adhered to the German cause, while living in Germany during the Second World War. The commission of the treasonable act was beyond doubt, but

17 Foster *Crown Law* p 183.
18 It will be recalled that the United Kingdom (then of Great Britain and Ireland) did not come into being until 1800: see Chapter 6, above.
19 [1946] AC 347, [1946] 1 All ER 186.

the accused was in fact a citizen of the United States of America. Nevertheless the jurisdiction of the English courts was held to be valid because he had obtained a British passport by false representations, and had renewed it shortly before the outbreak of war. Yet he had left no family or belongings of any kind in this country, and the passport was not even found in his possession. The House of Lords came to its decision by a majority, Lords Simonds, Macmillan and Wright concurring with the speech of Lord Jowitt LC, while only Lord Porter dissented on the ground that the question whether Joyce was making use of his passport at the time of his broadcasts had not been drawn to the attention of the jury. Thus the principle in the judges' resolution of 1707 would seem to have been extended, and the decision is of the binding authority of the House of Lords, even though it has not infrequently been criticised. It is perhaps possible to suggest one reason for the decision which was not considered significant by the courts, namely that England was the locus of the crime, for although the treasonable acts were committed in Germany they would have had little point unless they were actually heard by listeners to the wireless broadcasts in England.

Apart from the law of treason and of certain other offences against the state, an alien in the United Kingdom enjoys full civic rights, provided his own country is at peace with the United Kingdom, although he may not own or have a share in a British ship or aircraft, nor may he vote or stand as a candidate in Parliamentary or local elections. The Crown may probably exclude aliens from the country whenever it wishes, under its prerogative right, but in fact this is usually done, where necessary, by statutory provisions. Powers of internment and deportation are usually provided for by Act of Parliament. Enemy aliens can be arrested and imprisoned at common law, and they have no right to apply for a writ of habeas corpus against the Crown, or to bring civil actions, although they are permitted to defend civil actions or criminal prosecutions against them, and to appeal against adverse decisions of trial courts. There is legislation to control immigration to the United Kingdom from other parts of the Commonwealth, and to provide for deportation in certain cases.

These provisions were considerably strengthened by the Immigration Act 1971, but the law is in fact similar to that enforced by many Commonwealth countries. Powers of extradition are provided for by reciprocal treaties with various countries, whereby the United Kingdom government generally agrees (the exact agreement depends on the terms of each treaty) to hand over to such states any persons, whether British or not, either accused of or found guilty of committing any offences covered by the Extradition Act 1989. This Act covers most criminal offences, except those which are of a political nature. Thus no extradition will be allowed where the case is really one of an individual claiming political asylum against an oppressive regime.[20] But the Suppression of Terrorism Act 1978 restricts the possibility of terrorists evading extradition by pleading that their crimes are political offences. Again, no extradition will be allowed where the accused has already been tried in the United Kingdom for the offence.

III DUTIES OF THE CITIZEN IN THE UNITED KINGDOM

In the main body of this chapter the limitations upon the fundamental freedoms of the individual have been sketched. It is unnecessary to consider in any detail the constitutional duties of such individuals, because it can be appreciated that wherever the law has provided for a restriction upon full liberty it is the duty of all persons to obey that law. Similarly in respect of such freedom as remains after the restrictions upon it have been conceded, it is the duty of all persons to respect the individual liberties of others. Thus, to sum up, the laws of the United Kingdom provide for negative restrictions upon the safeguards for the constitutional rights of the individual. Such residuary rights must be respected by all persons,

---

20   As in *R v Governor of Brixton Prison, ex p Kolczynski* [1955] 1 QB 540, [1955] 1 All ER 31.

and can normally only be altered by Act of Parliament.[1] There is at once a privilege to enjoy these rights, and a complementary duty to respect them and to obey the law.

FURTHER READING

A. V. Dicey *Introduction to the Study of the Law of the Constitution* (10th edn, by E. C. S. Wade, 1959)

Roscoe Pound *The Development of Constitutional Guarantees of Liberty* (1957)

I. Brownlie *The Law Relating to Public Order and National Security* (2nd edn, 1981)

H. Street *Freedom, the Individual and the Law* (6th edn by G. Robertson, 1989)

D. Williams *Not in the Public Interest* (1965)

D. Williams *Keeping the Peace* (1967)

L. H. Leigh *Police Powers in England and Wales* (2nd edn, 1985)

I. N. Stevens and D. C. M. Yardley *The Protection of Liberty* (1982)

S. H. Bailey, D. J. Harris and B. L. Jones *Civil Liberties: Cases and Materials* (4th edn, 1995)

C. Palley *The United Kingdom and Human Rights* (1991).

---

1 Two other possible, though rarer, methods are delegated legislation (see Chapter 10, below) and judicial decisions. As regards the latter method, it is arguable that courts only develop, rather than change, the law. This is perhaps a question of interpretation: see above, *Elias v Pasmore* [1934] 2 KB 164, 103 LJKB 223; and *Thomas v Sawkins* [1935] 2 KB 249, 104 LJKB 572.

Chapter 8

The Church

Complete religious toleration is practised throughout the United Kingdom and the British Isles, and citizens are free to join or support any religious sect they wish. The sole limitation upon the scope given to all religious bodies is that provided by the criminal law of the land. For example, although members of certain Eastern religions are permitted by their faith to practise polygamy, the contraction of a polygamous marriage in the British Isles amounts to the crime of bigamy; and it is no defence to such a charge that any second ceremony of marriage was performed according to bona fide religious beliefs.

Of the many churches which maintain a following in the British Isles, however, two occupy a certain more privileged position than others, namely the Church of England (Episcopalian) and the Church of Scotland (Presbyterian). These two churches are said to be 'established' churches, although this is not really a technical term and it does not imply that any other religious bodies, whether Christian or not, are in any way discouraged. In particular the Roman Catholic Church has many adherents, whilst several non-conformist churches, notably the Methodist, Baptist and English United Reformed Churches, have widespread national organisations, as has also the Episcopalian or Anglican Church in Scotland. Again, there are many adherents to the Jewish faith in the United Kingdom. The Church of Ireland (Anglican) was 'disestablished' in 1869 by the Irish Church Act, as was also the Church of England in Wales by the Welsh Church Act 1914, and thus they occupy a similar position in the eyes of the law to all other non-privileged religious bodies in the British Isles. It will be recalled from Chapter 3, however, that priests of the Roman Catholic Church and clergy of the Church of Ireland are barred from membership of the House of Commons, as are also clergy of the Church of England and ministers of the Church of Scotland.

The effect of 'establishment' differs slightly in each of the cases of the two churches concerned, and it is perhaps best to examine them separately.

I THE CHURCH OF ENGLAND

The modern position of the protestant Church of England dates from the reign of Queen Elizabeth I, and in particular from the Act of Supremacy (1558) and the Act of Uniformity 1558, and its status was ratified in the Act of Union 1706. In a sense the Church was recognised by the state as being that which in its opinion truly taught the Christian faith. As has been mentioned in Chapter 4, the monarch must be in communion with the Church of England,[1] and the monarch's accession declaration and coronation oath, and the whole form of the coronation ceremony, and of certain other ceremonial occasions, is according to the beliefs of the Church of England. Archbishops and Bishops of the Church sit in the House of Lords,[2] whereas no other church is officially so represented, although any priest or minister of the Church of England or any other church who is also a peer may of course sit in the Lords. But perhaps the greatest effect of establishment has been that the decrees of the Church are of legal authority throughout England. Its legislative body is now the General Synod, instituted by the Synodical Government Measure 1969, and consisting of Bishops, clergy and laity. Any enactment which the Synod has decided to sponsor is formulated as a 'Measure', which is then submitted to Parliament for approval, such approval, if obtained, being given by simple

1   Bill of Rights 1689, Coronation Oath Act 1688, and Act of Settlement 1700.
2   See Chapter 3, above.

affirmative resolution of each House of Parliament. Once a Measure has passed Parliament it takes effect as if it were an Act of Parliament, but it applies directly only to the Church of England, and will affect other persons or bodies only negatively or indirectly. The work of the General Synod is assisted by 43 diocesan synods.

The executive organisation of the Church is according to a hierarchy, with Archbishops and Bishops as the superior authorities, priests and deacons as the lower orders, and with the monarch as 'Supreme Governor', though with no spiritual jurisdiction.[3] Many priests and deacons will, however, occupy posts of special ecclesiastical significance within a Bishop's diocese or within a local parish. Ecclesiastical courts of the Church of England are no longer of such general legal importance as they used to be before the middle of the nineteenth century, when they had competence in such matters as testamentary succession and matrimonial causes. Nowadays they have jurisdiction over internal ecclesiastical law only, usually concerning the interpretation of doctrine on the particular clerical behaviour of a clergyman. The hierarchy, composition and procedure of these courts was modernised by the Ecclesiastical Jurisdiction Measure 1963 (1963 No 1), but a final appeal in all matters still lies to the Judicial Committee of the Privy Council.

II THE CHURCH OF SCOTLAND

The Church of Scotland is a protestant church, but with a non-episcopalian form of government. It received recognition in Scotland by a series of Acts of the Scottish Parliament before the union with England, and in the Treaty of Union 1706, and the ratifying statutes of the two Parliaments, the establishment of both the Church of England and the Church of Scotland was guaranteed permanently for the future, although, as we have pointed out in Chapter 2, Parliament cannot bind itself absolutely for the future as far as statutes affecting England are

3   Act of Supremacy (1558).

concerned: as we have seen the position may be different in Scotland. The special constitutional position of the Church of Scotland does not conflict with the status of the Church of England, for the latter is established within England only. Whereas the Church of England has as its 'Supreme Governor' the monarch, who is also temporal head of the state, the Church of Scotland claims to exercise unfettered spiritual sovereignty, and thus to possess a jurisdiction jure divino coordinate with that of the state. The legislative Acts of its General Assembly are regarded as statutes of the realm, needing neither parliamentary approval nor the royal assent.

The organisation of the clergy of the Church of Scotland is not founded upon a hierarchical system, and thus there are no Bishops or other superior clergymen of the Church. The Church is governed by a hierarchy of courts, Kirk Session, Presbytery, Synod and General Assembly, in all of which ordained clergymen, called ministers, and lay elders have equal place. Each is presided over by a clerical Moderator, and the Moderator of the General Assembly ranks as the leader of the Church during his year of office. Although the monarch is not the 'Supreme Governor' of the Church, he or his commissioner has the right to attend sessions of the General Assembly of the Church,[4] and it is conventional for him to attend services of the Church of Scotland when in Scotland. The Church courts enforce church discipline, etc in much the same way as in the Church of England. The Church is entitled to legislate for itself, and does so normally through resolutions of its General Assembly[5] which, as has been pointed out above, do not require the approval of Parliament. It is perhaps for this reason that there is no direct representation of the Church in the House of Lords, as there is in the case of the Church of England.

It may therefore be seen that both the Church of England and the Church of Scotland maintain privileged positions in the constitutional system of the United Kingdom, but

4   Act 1592, cap 8, of the Scottish Parliament (often referred to as 'the Charter of the Church'), which is still in force.
5   Church of Scotland Act 1921.

in effect their authority as established churches is restricted to England and Scotland respectively, and all churches are really of equal status in Wales and Northern Ireland. Disestablishment of the two Churches is a possibility for the future which is discussed from time to time both outside and within them, but no positive proposals on these lines are imminent.

FURTHER READING

Sir Thomas Taylor 'Church and State in Scotland' [1957] Juridical Review 121
R. King Murray 'The Constitutional Position of the Church of Scotland' [1958] PL 155
E. Garth Moore *An Introduction to English Canon Law* (1967).

Part II

Principles of English Administrative Law

Chapter 9

The Nature of
Administrative Law

In the second part of this book we are only concerned with English law, rather than the general law of the United Kingdom. This is because, unlike other parts of constitutional law, administrative law has been built up in each of the component countries of the union as a separate and individual entity. No direct and apposite comparison can be made between the administrative laws of England and Scotland or Northern Ireland although it is true to say once more that the law of Northern Ireland is not greatly dissimilar from that of England.

The old fallacy propagated, probably partly unwittingly, by Dicey in his celebrated lectures, first published in 1885,[1] that there is no such thing as administrative law in England, has died hard. Dicey was in fact at pains to draw a distinction between England, where all aspects of human behaviour are subject to control and review in the ordinary courts of the land, and France, where a separate body of courts existed for the purpose of determining disputes between citizens and any part of the executive arm of government. This distinction was, and still is, perfectly valid. But it was unfortunate that Dicey went on to draw the conclusion that administrative courts of France must necessarily favour the administration against any individual wherever a dispute exists between them, and that therefore the French *droit administratif* offends against the desirable principle of equality before the law. Dicey's view was drawn upon time and again as a basis

1   See Chapter 7, above.

for national pride, and especially for the making of satisfactory comparisons between our own fair system of law and what has been alleged to be an unfair system across the channel in France.

Curiously some of our best judges have not been immune from the contagion first started by Dicey. Thus Lord Denning in 1970 opined:[2] 'Our English law does not allow a public officer to shelter behind a *droit administratif.*' And Lord Reid six years earlier said:[3] 'We do not have a developed system of administrative law — perhaps because until fairly recently we did not need it...' though it is clear from the context of the latter pronouncement that he was mainly concerned to stress that all types of administrative action in England are subject to review by the ordinary, rather than special, courts which after all was the same perfectly valid premise from which Dicey started. A little thought will inevitably point to the conclusion that a body of law in England must always have existed to regulate relations between the citizen and the state, whatever the nature of that law may have been, and any suggestion that governmental power has only arisen in recent decades is insupportable. The steady march of governmental power to cover almost all aspects of the citizen's life was not just a product of the First World War and the profound changes wrought upon society as its result. There were many signs even in the nineteenth century of state intervention and the gradual growth of government control. Maitland in 1888 wrote:[4] 'We are becoming a much governed nation, governed by all manner of councils and boards and officers, central and local, high and low, exercising the powers which have been committed to them by modern statutes.' But the rate of progress towards such control has gained momentum most markedly in the period starting with the Second World War, and it is no exaggeration to say that the power of governmental intervention today bears very little resemblance to its modest predecessor of a century or so ago.

2   *Ministry of Housing and Local Government v Sharp* [1970] 2 QB 223 at 226.
3   *Ridge v Baldwin* [1964] AC 40 at 72.
4   *Constitutional History of England* (1955 reprint) p 501.

The kernel of the whole subject of administrative law is the control of power within its lawful compass. Provided this essential umpiring function of the law is kept in mind, it is of much less consequence to attempt to formulate an acceptable definition of administrative law. Indeed no generally agreed definition has ever been put forward, and this is partly because the law operates positively as well as negatively. The law is employed not just to disqualify unlawful exercise of power, but also to compel the performance of legal duties which have been neglected.

Apart from a small, though significant, reservoir of power left by the 1689 Revolution settlement to the prerogative of the Crown (and always subject at any time to removal or restriction by statute), administrative power is invariably to be traced to statutory authorisation. In a sense, therefore, the function of the courts is little more than one of statutory interpretation. But such a conclusion would overlook many of the subtleties of the English legal system. Judges have not infrequently denied that they make law, but commentators have learned to take such modest assertions with a pinch of salt. Although courts are bound by statute, and thus must apply any rule established either by or under the authority of Act of Parliament, this has not deterred them from applying such important common law presumptions as the rules of natural justice (which will be discussed in Chapter 12 of this book), and by so doing interpreting the relevant legislation in such a way as to surprise Parliament.

The 'superior' character of the courts of the level of High Court and above is important, for whichever way one turns this judicial supervisory power, inherent in the superior courts, is inescapable. Some may deplore it, and politicians not infrequently chafe under it, but it is probable that there is no acceptable substitute which could be found for it in a democratic country. To allow politicians, elected to office through the vagaries of the electorate's majority wishes at any one time, to be judges of their own ambit of authority for a period of up to five years before the next General Election could spell tyranny, at least in the short term. Where so much power in the modern state reposes in the administration, an impartial umpire between the conflicting interests of the administration and the citizen is essential, and such an umpire must be immune from the threat of dismissal as a result of deciding any issue in a manner which may be unpopular with the government. Only the judges of our superior courts, with their security of tenure established by the Act of Settlement 1700, meet these requirements. No one has yet suggested any more suitable person or body to act as umpire, and it is submitted therefore that it is an essential part of our administrative law to recognise and support the power of review that resides in the judges.

This is not to say, however, that the purpose of administrative law is to stifle administration. By the proper exercise of the courts' supervisory power illegal power is excised, but this leaves the legal use of power untouched. Thus the practice of administrative law should lead to the assistance of good administration, and positively encourage administrative powers to be exercised only validly. Above all, administrative law amounts to the rules employed by the courts to enable them to achieve a practical application of constitutional law.

FURTHER READING

P. Cane *An Introduction to Administrative Law* (2nd edn, 1992)
N. Hawke *An Introduction to Administrative Law* (1984)
L. N. Brown and J. S. Bell *French Administrative Law* (4th edn, 1993)
J. Schwarze *European Administrative Law* (1992).

Chapter 10

Subordinate Legislation

It has been seen in Chapters 2 and 3 that in the United Kingdom the power to legislate is vested in Parliament at Westminster. This power is supplemented by the adjudicatory function of the law courts, which apply and interpret Acts of Parliament as may be necessary, but which also follow the rules established by the method of case precedent wherever no statute law is relevant.[1] But there is still another method of law-making, known as delegated or subordinate legislation, which stems from the position of Parliament as sovereign body, even though it is not a manifestation of the direct functioning of Parliament. Wherever an Act of Parliament provides that any government department, local authority, the Crown, or any individual or body shall have the power to make regulations or orders that shall have the force of law, that statute is regarded as laying down a method of creating delegated legislation, and any regulations or orders made under such powers take effect as if part of the 'parent' Act,[2] provided that they conform to the limitations expressed in that parent Act.[3] The power to legislate in this way may, however, be conferred only by an Act of Parliament, or, more rarely, by the royal prerogative. The term 'subordinate legislation' really includes law-making under the power of the royal prerogative, discussed above in Chapter 4, as where the Crown legislates by Proclamation or Order

1   See Chapter 5, above.
2   *Institute of Patent Agents v Lockwood* [1894] AC 347.
3   *Minister of Health v R, ex p Yaffe* [1931] AC 494, 100 LJKB 306.

in Council for newly conquered or ceded colonies. But *delegated* legislation, properly so called, may only be created under statutory powers, and it is this subject which it is our main purpose to consider in the present chapter. Nevertheless, whether the authority for subordinate legislation be, in any particular instance, a statute or the royal prerogative, the person or body empowered to create the subordinate legislation is usually a part of the Crown, as we shall see presently, and thus the law concerning the effect and control of this legislation is administrative law. It may also be noted in passing that, in the case of delegated legislation, the parent Act may provide for sub-delegation of powers conferred, but that sub-delegation is only lawful if authorised expressly or by necessary implication by the enabling Act.

The necessity for the existence of subordinate legislation is primarily dictated by the exigencies of modern life in a democratic community. An enormous amount of regulation is required to ensure orderly and just provision for the needs of all citizens. There is far too much for Parliament alone to deal with in detail, and in any case some regulations have to be brought into force at very short notice in view of sudden changes of, for example, economic conditions. Parliament would be unlikely to be able to pass a Bill to meet such conditions sufficiently quickly, as its immediate programme of business may already be full. Again, the need for certain new regulations is often appreciated by government departments, which have special means of knowing the conditions prevailing in the country or the world in its own field of interest, but may not be apparent to MPs who are not members of the government or of that department, and who may belong to an Opposition party which would feel bound to oppose the measure for political reasons, as in the case of a Bill before the House. It has therefore become increasingly recognised by responsible persons during the past half-century that discretionary powers must be vested by Parliament in specific persons or bodies, though in most cases with careful safeguards to prevent abuse of such power. Although Lord Hewart severely criticised the growth of delegated legislation in his book *The New*

Despotism, published in 1929 while the author was still in office as Lord Chief Justice of England, the fears that had prompted the publication were soothed by the later 'Report of the Committee on Ministers' Powers' in 1932.[4] The result of this Report was that consistent opposition to the existence of the powers became less frequent, and the energies of those who had previously felt their danger were directed into reinforcing the safeguards surrounding the exercise of such powers.

TYPES OF DELEGATED LEGISLATION

In effect it is open to Parliament to create any delegated legislative power it wishes, in whatever form and vested in whatever person or body it cares, for this is a power implicit in the sovereignty of Parliament. For example, it has sometimes conferred a power to impose taxation, or even to modify or adapt the parent Act or other Acts of Parliament, though Parliament will not normally do this without good reason. The most usual types of delegated legislation which have been provided for by statute in the past can be tabulated without great difficulty, and there is no reason to believe that Parliament will wish in the future to depart from its established practice. The main varieties are:

(1)   local authority by-laws. Thus in statutes creating local authorities or in any way altering the powers of such authorities that already exist it is common to include a section or sections empowering the authorities to make local by-laws or regulations which shall have effect as binding law upon everyone in the district. An account of the system of local government will be seen in Chapter 14 below;

(2)   public corporation by-laws. The nature of public corporations has already been described in Chapter 4, and the power of these corporations to make by-laws for the regulation of their business, employees, etc is similarly usually included in statutes creating them or altering their powers;

4   Cmnd 4060.

(3)   Rules of the Supreme Court and of the County Court, etc. Rules committees are sometimes set up by statute specifically empowered to make rules concerning the practice and procedure of the courts already described in Chapter 5;

(4)   regulations made by the European Commission or the Council of Ministers;

(5)   ministerial or departmental regulations. These, together with the delegated legislation in category (6) below, are the most common and widely used of delegated legislative powers, and they are called statutory instruments. This is why delegated legislation falls under the heading of administrative law, even though in theory such a power to create legislation may be conferred by Parliament upon anyone, and not just upon the administration;

(6)   Orders made by the Monarch in Council. These are often similar in nature to ministerial or departmental regulations, but they are generally of wider national importance, and the authority for their creation may stem from the royal prerogative as well as from Parliament. Instead of being formulated entirely by the minister or government department primarily concerned, without any outside help or advice being necessary, they may originate as the embodiment of government policy, but most receive the assent of the monarch in the Privy Council before they may come into effect. In practice the distinction between Orders in Council and ministerial or departmental regulations is perhaps not vital, because a normal meeting of the Privy Council will consist of the monarch, three or four ministers who are Privy Councillors, including the Lord President of the Council, and the Clerk to the Privy Council, but the procedure does at least ensure slightly more publicity and the possibility of second thoughts on the part of the government.

It will be realised that in the case of the last two types of delegated legislation any powers which are conferred by statute will enable the government of the day to enforce its policy decisions as being law, which could result in a grave abuse of the trust imposed in the executive. But the responsibility of ministers to Parliament is an important check on any such tendency, even though it would probably be possible for the government to force any Bill embodying its desires through Parliament by means of its party majority if it really wished. The executive control of, or at least predominance of power in, Parliament would lead to the same policy becoming law, but the advantages of delegated legislation from the point of view of the government are those of speed, especially in emergencies or in war-time, the ability to deal with a technical subject-matter without having to explain the whole issue painstakingly to Parliament, and flexibility, in that regulations may be made, altered or rescinded as and when it is thought appropriate and without unnecessary delay. To set against these advantages it may be urged that the lack of general publicity consequent upon dealing with such matters in the ordinary legislative form in Parliament may be harmful and unfair, but certain safeguards have been brought into being to counteract any such undesirable trends.

Parliamentary safeguards

LAYING BEFORE PARLIAMENT

In order to provide that Parliament shall at least have cognisance of such delegated legislation as is of national importance, namely Orders in Council and ministerial and departmental regulations, the enabling Act very often now provides that any regulations made under the terms of the Act, or any draft Orders in Council which are proposed, shall be laid before Parliament or before one or other of the Houses of Parliament.[5] In many cases there is no express power vested in the House or Houses by the enabling Act to vote on the matter, and thus the 'laying before' is purely for the information of members; and in

5   To the author's knowledge there has never yet been a statutory provision that an instrument should be laid before the House of Lords only, but in principle there is no reason why such a provision should not be enacted.

some cases indeed the delegated legislation may already have come into force. Members may, however, ask parliamentary questions concerning the instrument, even though it is not possible for the House to vote on the matter directly. On the other hand it is sometimes provided that the regulation shall not come into force or continue in force unless an affirmative resolution of one or both of the Houses shall have been passed, or else that the regulation or order shall become or remain law unless one or other House annuls it by a negative note within a specific time. It must be emphasised that the specific kinds of 'laying before' under the principle discussed here may theoretically be limitless in number, because in each case the nature of the control depends upon the terms of the parent Act. But the Report of the Select Committee on Delegated Legislation in 1953 declares that there are only three types of 'laying before' in practice, namely those already mentioned:

(1)   the laying of an instrument before either or both of the Houses for information, Parliament having no power under the terms of the parent Act to vote on the instrument;
(2)   the laying of an instrument before either or both of the Houses, with the requirement of an affirmative resolution to bring it into force or to continue it in force; and
(3)   the laying of an instrument before either or both of the Houses, with the possibility (but no requirement) of a negative vote which would annul it or prevent it coming into force.

THE SCRUTINY COMMITTEES

A Special Orders Committee was set up in the House of Lords in 1925, charged with the duty to scrutinise and report upon instruments requiring an affirmative resolution of the House before coming into effect or continuing in force, ie instruments laid before the House which fall under heading (2) above, but not those falling under (1) or (3). A Select Committee on Statutory Instr-uments was also set up in the Commons in 1944 as a delayed implementation of one of the recommendations of the Committee on Ministers' Powers.[6] 'Statutory instruments' is a collective term which covers all Orders in Council made under statutory powers (as opposed to those made under the prerogative power), together with such ministerial or departmental regulations as may be designated statutory instruments by their enabling Acts, but not other varieties of delegated legislation. The Committee was empowered to scrutinise a wider range of instruments, and to report upon many matters of form, though not of policy. It is perhaps a tribute to departmental integrity and conscientiousness that the Committee only found it necessary to draw the attention of the House to a few out of the total number of instruments referred to it, but it was also wasteful of time for the two Houses to maintain separate scrutiny committees.

In 1973 these two committees were in effect merged to form a new Joint Committee on Statutory Instruments which is charged with the duty to consider all instruments or draft instruments laid before both Houses of Parliament. It must report to both Houses, and draw their attention to any such secondary legislation which (i) imposes a tax on the public, (ii) is made in pursuance of an enactment containing specific provisions excluding it from challenge in the courts, (iii) purports to have retrospective effect where there is no express authority in the enabling statute, (iv) has been unduly delayed in publication or laying before Parliament, (v) has come into operation before being laid before Parliament and there has been unjustifiable delay in informing the Speaker of the delay, (vi) is of doubtful *vires*, ie there is some doubt whether it is properly within the powers laid down by statute, or makes some unusual or unexpected use of the powers conferred by the enabling statute, (vii) calls for any special reason of form or purport for elucidation, or (viii) is defective in its drafting. The older Select Committee on Statutory Instruments still remains to scrutinise those few instruments which, under the terms of the enabling Acts, are to be laid only before the Commons. But otherwise the Joint Committee has

6   Cmd 4060 (1932) pp 67-69.

superseded the older bodies. Further, the Commons at the same time set up a Standing Committee of the House to consider statutory instruments and draft instruments referred to it on the question of merits.

In 1974 the Commons also set up the Select Committee on European Secondary Legislation, and the Lords set up the Select Committee on the European Communities. These Committees are charged with the task of singling out and bringing to the attention of Parliament the more important Community proposals. The Commons Committee in any case makes a general report to the House on Community business every six months. Provided these Committees make their views clear in sufficient time, a debate on a matter of urgency or importance can take place in Parliament before the Council of Ministers makes a final decision.

OTHER PARLIAMENTARY SAFEGUARDS

Additional parliamentary safeguards are inherent in the power of members of either House to ask questions concerning, inter alia, delegated legislation, to call for a debate (probably through the Leader of the Opposition), and even in extreme cases to move the censure of the government. Such procedures may be particularly useful in respect of delegated legislation in the form of statutory instruments which only have to be laid before Parliament, or one of the Houses of Parliament, for information, and where consequently there is no possibility of a direct affirmative or negative resolution, ie instruments falling under heading (1) above.

Judicial safeguards

If any delegated legislation, of whatever kind, is formulated contrary to the terms of its enabling Act, or in excess of the powers conferred, then it may be challenged in the courts as being ultra vires (outside the powers conferred by) the enabling Act. The actual methods whereby such challenge may be pursued will be considered in the next chapter, but for the present it is sufficient to say that although delegated legislation takes effect as if it is part of its parent Act,[7] and is thus of statutory force, yet this result does not come about unless the delegated legislation is intra vires, that is, properly formulated according to the terms of the Act.[8] Although Acts of Parliament are immune from judicial challenge, delegated legislation can be challenged in the courts on the ground that it is ultra vires, and this may include the power of the courts to hold delegated legislation invalid because it is unreasonable.[9]

Political safeguards

It may sometimes be provided in the parent Act that the minister concerned should consult interested bodies or an Advisory Committee before issuing regulations. Again, the Statutory Instruments Act 1946 provides that all statutory instruments shall be published by the Stationery Office after they have been made. Where any statutory instrument is required to be laid before Parliament after being made, the published copies must contain the date on which it came or will come into operation. Such provisions are useful in ensuring a reasonable amount of consultation before committing a policy to become law, and in making provision for any interested party to be able to read the terms of the instrument concerned, but they are perhaps not strictly methods of control. But any person charged with an offence under a statutory instrument has a good defence if he can prove that the instrument had not at the time of the offence been published by the Stationery Office, unless reasonable steps had been taken to bring the instrument to the notice of the public, the person charged or persons likely to be affected by it.[10]

7   *Institute of Patent Agents v Lockwood* [1894] AC 347.
8   *Minister of Health v R, ex p Yaffe* [1931] AC 494, 100 LJKB 306; *R v Halliday, ex p Zadig* [1917] AC 260. See also *Allingham v Minister of Agriculture* [1948] 1 All ER 780, where an invalid sub-delegation of power had been made.
9   See, eg, *Kruse v Johnson* [1898] 2 QB 91.
10   Statutory Instruments Act 1946, s 3(2).

It is possible that some additional method ought to be devised to bring instruments to the notice of the general public more readily than by publications of the Stationery Office, although it may be unrealistic to imagine that an apathetic populace would avail itself of such wider publicity. The present provision for publication of statutory instruments does at least provide for *some* publicity of the measures concerned, and thus it may facilitate one final safeguard against unwarranted acts of the executive, namely that of public opinion. Great unpopularity may make it politically expedient for the government to change its policy and to rescind any regulations already made.[11] This is essentially a topic outside the scope of a lawyer, but it is possible that such a political safeguard is a real supplement to the existing legal safeguards, and that it ensures that the legitimate purposes of delegated legislation are not misused to any serious extent.

FURTHER READING

Sir William Wade *Administrative Law* (7th edn, 1994)
J. F. Garner *Administrative Law* (7th edn, 1989)
D. C. M. Yardley *Principles of Administrative Law* (2nd edn, 1986)
Sir Carleton K. Allen *Law and Orders* (3rd edn, 1965)
D. Foulkes *Administrative Law* (7th edn, 1990)
J. Beatson and M. H. Matthews *Administrative Law: Cases and Materials* (2nd edn, 1989).

---

11   An instance of the effect of public opinion (although not a case of delegated legislation) was the agitation leading to the setting up of a Public Inquiry into the Crichel Down affair in 1954; see 'Public Inquiry ordered by the Minister of Agriculture into the disposal of land at Crichel Down' Cmnd 9176 (1954), discussed below in Chapter 13.

Chapter 11

Tribunals and Inquiries

It is a notable feature of our public life in the present century that no longer is all, or even the great bulk, of our judicial business carried out by judges in the ordinary courts of the land. Progressively and inexorably a considerable proportion of the decision-making which in former centuries would as a matter of course have had to be discharged by the courts, if indeed the problems at issue counted among those which were recognised as justiciable, has been handed over to specially constituted bodies of citizens from all walks of life who sit in judgment upon their fellow-citizens in the so-called administrative tribunals. This appellation is to some extent unfortunate, because the powers of the various tribunals are mainly judicial rather than administrative. 'Special tribunals' might well be a less misleading description, but the traditional term is so well established that it would only serve to confuse to attempt in this book to adopt any more accurate title for them.

It has frequently been asked why there is any need to have such tribunals, particularly since administration is normally in the hands of the Crown and its servants or agents, while judicial decisions would be obtainable through the ordinary courts. The reason is that under modern circumstances, just as there is far too much legislation required at any given time for Parliament to be able to cope with the load (so that we are bound to need delegated legislation, as has been discussed in the last chapter), so also there are too many problems of mixed law and administration, or of law concerned with the administration, for the courts to be able to deal with them effectively and speedily. We have only to realise the ramifications of one major aspect of modern life, the welfare state, to understand how the courts cannot possibly provide an adequate or suitable judicial service for its purposes. Under current welfare state legislation, virtually all of which dates from the period since the Second World War, there is provision on the one hand for the collection on a compulsory basis of insurance contributions from all those living in the country who earn income, and on the other hand for the payment of a whole battery of different types of benefit covered by this compulsory insurance scheme. Qualification for the payment of any one of such benefits will depend upon a variety of factors, including the relevant contribution record or conditions; whether the circumstance intended to be covered by the benefit has actually occurred; and whether the claim was made within the requisite time limit, and if not whether the proviso that a claim made out of time may be allowed if continuous good cause for the delay can be proved has been satisfied. These are only a few of the problems which arise constantly under the welfare state insurance scheme, but all require a judicial-type investigation or trial before the relevant legal answer can be arrived at. Sometimes the problems at issue are complicated by questions as to the eligibility of dependants to enable claimants to obtain increases of benefit, or, in the case of unemployment benefit (to be replaced in 1996 by a jobseeker's allowance), the question whether a claimant is disqualified from benefit because he has lost his employment by virtue of his involvement as an interested party in a trade dispute at his place of employment. In a nation which has become accustomed to an overall unemployment figure approaching three millions it is clear that the burden of judicial decision related to unemployment benefit alone is heavy.

The welfare state provides perhaps the most obvious and weighty example of a field of administrative law which requires a special decision-making process outside the ordinary courts. But there are many other areas of modern life which throw up a similar need. Problems of law or mixed law and administration inevitably arise from the process of civil aviation licensing, the fixing of rents in privately let accommodation, council tax valuation appeals, applications and references by patients under the Mental Health Act 1959 and later statutes, and allegations of unfair dismissal from employment; and these again are only examples taken virtually at random from a vast patchwork quilt of what Sir Carleton Allen called 'administrative jurisdiction'.[1] The courts could never cope with them unless they were greatly increased in number. But even such an expansion of the court system would not suffice, for the prime requirements in dealing with the problem arising in this whole area of administrative law are speed, cheapness, a special aptitude for the particular type of problems concerned (a quality which is provided for by the composition of each tribunal), lack of formality and forms, and the provision of a type of justice which often involves a fair degree of compromise, thus contrasting with the normal court decision whereby one party or the other becomes successful at the expense of the other.

Where it has been decided by Parliament to entrust the power to decide problems within the area of administrative law to some body which is independent of the administration, the task is normally given to an administrative tribunal. But the Crown still retains a considerable area of decision-making within its own hands, and exercises it through the decisions of ministers and secretaries of state. Yet even here it has long been recognised that a decision should only be made after first following a procedure which is intended to enable those who will be affected by the decision to make their views known; and this type of procedure is an inquiry. The most common inquiries are concerned with proposals which affect property rights. Thus inquiry procedures are used in connection with schemes to create new towns, or in relation to appeals to the secretary of state against refusal by a local planning authority of proposals to develop land, and where there are proposals to acquire private land compulsorily for housing, or in order to build airports or new motorways. The actual inquiry is conducted by an inspector, whose duty it is to

1   C. K. Allen *Administrative Jurisdiction* (1956).

allow all objectors a fair chance to put their case, after which he must make a report and recommendations to the minister. In essence this process is intended to enable the mind of the minister who decides a particular issue to be properly informed before he comes to his decision, while not requiring him necessarily to arrive at his determination in accordance with the weight of the evidence brought to his attention.

I THE DEVELOPMENT OF ADMINISTRATIVE TRIBUNALS

Many tribunals have in the past been severely criticised, largely, it is submitted, because of the previously widespread practice of not publishing their decisions or giving reasons for their decisions, and also partly in ignorance of the valuable work which is done by tribunals with little or no fuss or publicity. It is, however, true to say that certain tribunals have on occasions committed serious errors either of law or judgement, and these have received publicity. Criticism of administrative tribunals was among the reasons leading to the setting up of a Committee on Administrative Tribunals and Enquiries, under the chairmanship of Sir Oliver Franks, which reported in July 1957.[2] The majority of the recommendations of this Committee were accepted by the major political parties, many were implemented by government departments as matters of policy, and a Tribunals and Inquiries Act 1958 was passed to provide for the enactment of such of the recommendations as required immediate statutory effect. This statute, as amended and consolidating numerous other enactments relevant to tribunals and inquiries, has now been re-enacted as the Tribunals and Inquiries Act 1992.

Detailed criticisms of administrative tribunals have in the main been three-fold:

(1)   that they are totally unnecessary. This criticism was probably finally answered by the findings of the

2   Cmnd 218.

Franks Committee that they are absolutely necessary, and even desirable, in modern conditions,[3] though some methods of control should be strengthened. The Committee also emphasised that the three great principles which should always be followed by such tribunals were those of openness, fairness and impartiality. On the whole these principles have usually been observed in the past, and it is clear that they are carefully followed today;

(2)   that a system of entirely separate administrative courts should be set up, rather like the French system of courts concerned only with the *droit administratif,* or alternatively that there should be set up an Administrative Appeal Court or an Administrative Division of the High Court, to hear appeals direct in all cases from administrative tribunals. The Franks Committee decided against these suggestions, but it did, as we shall see presently, recommend an extension of the possibilities of direct appeal. Despite the Franks Committee there remained for 25 years a considerable body of opinion among English lawyers favouring at least the creation of an Administrative Division of the High Court.[4] It seems, however, that these views have now been substantially met by the setting up in 1982 of a special panel of judges of the Queen's Bench Division to sit in the Divisional Court when it is hearing any case involving administrative law;

(3)   that all administrative procedure should be standardised, as in the United States of America, where a federal Administrative Procedure Act was passed in 1946. This Act has been only partly successful, because of the great diversity of work covered by administrative agencies, and the Franks Committee probably extracted the value from this criticism without adopting it in toto by recommending the setting up of a Council of Tribunals to keep a watchful eye upon the procedure of the various tribunals, and to recommend changes where it thinks fit.

3   Cmnd 218 (1957), paras 403, 406.
4   See, eg, *Administration under Law* (a Report by Justice, 1971).

It is not usually necessary for a law student to have any detailed knowledge of the various types of tribunals unless he or she is studying the specialist subject covered. Fuller lists, including the detailed duties and powers of each tribunal, may be studied elsewhere.[5] In this book we are concerned only with principles, and it should be noted that tribunals may be of any kind at all. Whatever their composition or detailed powers they will be regarded as administrative tribunals provided that their functions in some way involve a consideration of the relationships of or disputes between the state and the individual.

Examples are the General Commissioners of Income Tax, the Lands Tribunal, Social Security Appeal Tribunals, Valuation and Community Charge Tribunals, and Mental Health Review Tribunals. There are also some tribunals which are set up to deal with disputes which arise between individuals, and which are in fact of little or no interest to the state as such so far as their individual decisions are concerned. Examples would be Rent Tribunals and Rent Assessment Committees. In some foreign countries, such as France, it is very doubtful whether this latter group of tribunals would be considered as dealing with anything outside the realm of ordinary private law,[6] but they are still regarded as administrative tribunals in this country because they deal with subjects which are outside the scope of the common law courts, and which are an integral part of the broad social policy of the country. Some tribunals can include High Court judges among their chairmen or members as for example the Employment Appeal Tribunal.

A number of matters concerning tribunals generally may be briefly noted:

(1)   following the Franks Committee recommendations, a Council on Tribunals now advises the Lord Chancellor as regards England and Wales and the Lord Advocate as regards Scotland upon the general supervision and procedure of tribunals and inquiries, and makes reports to Parliament upon its work;

5   See, eg, the Annual Reports of the Council on Tribunals.
6   See C. J. Hamson *Executive Discretion and Judicial Control: an Aspect of the Conseil d'Etat* (1954).

(2)   chairmen, and in certain other cases the members, of tribunals are often selected by the appropriate minister from a panel of persons appointed by the Lord Chancellor;

(3)   chairmen of tribunals generally have legal training;

(4)   legal representation is normally allowed, if required by any of the parties who appear before tribunals;

(5)   there is a full disclosure of all material facts to all parties before a tribunal hearing, and adequate notice of such a hearing is given;

(6)   hearings are held in public, unless public security is involved or intimate personal or financial matters, or professional capacity or reputation, are concerned;

(7)   reasons for decisions must be given, if requested;

(8)   the Franks Committee recommended that there should normally be an appellate tribunal to hear appeals on fact, law or the merits from any first instance tribunal, but that otherwise no special appeal tribunal or court should be set up. This particular recommendation has never yet been implemented. It is, however, submitted that it is hard to visualise any useful way in which appeals on *fact* can lie to an appellate tribunal without such an appeal developing into a simple rehearing of the issue which was heard below. If that were to happen the tribunal hearings would be robbed of their virtues of speed and cheapness. From such an appellate tribunal, when constituted, the Committee recommended that there should be an appeal on law only to the Divisional Court (or the Court of Session in Scotland). Although the Tribunals and Inquiries Act did not institute appeals to an appellate tribunal, it did provide for appeals on law to lie from most tribunals to the Divisional Court (or Court of Session). The effect of the enactment, therefore, is to provide for appeals on law to the court in the case of most of the tribunals from which such appeals did not already lie;[7]

7   See *Rule of Law* (Conservative Political Centre, 1955) Appendix, in which are listed the most important tribunals from which appeals of various kinds, either to a court or to another tribunal or to the minister, already lay before the Tribunals and Inquiries Act 1958 came into effect.

(9) appellate tribunals now usually publish selected decisions for the guidance of lower tribunals. Since the implementation of most of the Franks Committee's recommendations there is no longer any substantial reason for dissatisfaction with the powers and duties of tribunals. Nevertheless the independent Justice — All Souls Review of Administrative Law in the United Kingdom made a number of detailed recommendations for further improvement of the system when it reported in 1988.[8]

II THE DEVELOPMENT OF INQUIRIES

The main distinguishing feature between tribunals and inquiries is that the former type of body has conferred upon it the full power to determine the issue before it, whereas the latter has not. At an inquiry there will be a full investigation of the faults at issue but the eventual resolution of these matters need not necessarily accord with the balance of the evidence adduced at the inquiry, and is in any case provided by a minister or other authority outside the actual inquiry procedure.

The Franks Committee, which has already been referred to, was required to consider the system of both tribunals and inquiries, and a number of the reforms subsequently effected have concerned the latter. (It is curious that the Committee was asked to deal with 'Enquiries', whilst Parliament then legislated for 'Inquiries'!) The most far-reaching reform stems from the provision, now in the Tribunals and Inquiries Act 1992, that the Lord Chancellor may make rules regulating the procedure to be followed where any inquiries are held on behalf of a minister, and such rules have been made covering a number of the most common types of inquiry, particularly those held before a minister decides on the merits of appeals to him against local refusal of planning permission. These rules now specify the period of notice to be given before an inquiry is held, the procedure to be adopted at the inquiry, the form

8   Administrative Justice — Some Necessary Reforms.

of the inspector's report to the minister, and the way in which the minister's eventual decision, together with reasons, must be notified to the parties concerned. In particular it is provided that where a minister differs from the inspector on a finding of fact, or takes into account any new issue of fact, and is in consequence disposed to disagree with any recommendation made by the inspector, he must give the parties who appeared at the inquiry an opportunity of making representations or of having the inquiry reopened before he makes any decision contrary to the inspector's recommendations. It will be readily seen, therefore, that the ministers are far less free than they were before the Franks Committee reported to make decisions in this field which pay scant regard to the weight of evidence at prior inquiries. Perhaps the trend of greater control over the powers of ministers was in this area taken to its fullest extent by the provisions, in the Town and Country Planning Act 1968, for the final determination by the inspector himself of a number of appeals against the refusal of planning permission. This effectively removed the decision-making power from the minister altogether, even though the provision was really made to relieve the department of a flood of minor appeals.

In addition to its recommendations about tribunals the Justice — All Souls Review made a number of detailed suggestions for the improvement of inquiries, though they need not concern us here. Inquiries will remain controversial in the sense that they often deal with matters on which opinion and emotion can be highly charged — proposals for building on green field sites, for extending airports or for building nuclear power stations, and so on. But the overall scheme of inquiry procedure is generally accepted as satisfactory.

FURTHER READING

D. C. M. Yardley *Principles of Administrative Law* (2nd edn, 1986)
R. E. Wraith and P. Hutchesson *Administrative Tribunals* (1973)
Administrative Justice — Some Necessary Reforms

(Justice — All Souls Review of Administrative Law in the
United Kingdom, 1988)
J. F. McEldowney *Public Law* (1994)
The Annual Reports of the Council on Tribunals.

Chapter 12

The Control of Power

I GROUNDS FOR CONTROL

The primary ground upon which judicial review of administrative action may be based is that the jurisdiction of the authority concerned is defective. Once more, therefore, the issue in administrative law often boils down to one of statutory interpretation. This is at the heart of the doctrine of ultra vires, which has already been discussed in Chapter 10, but the ways in which the doctrine may be invoked are almost unlimited. If a validly created power is exercised by the wrong authority, the latter will have acted ultra vires. Again, if the right authority exercises the power excessively or against the wrong person or in some other unlawful way, then a court may similarly condemn the illegality. And there are countless possible variations. Even though a power is apparently exercised by the right authority, that authority may not have been properly appointed or constituted, or some fact which is a condition precedent to the possession of power may have been absent, or power may have been exercised in bad faith, unreasonably, for an improper purpose, or after taking irrelevant considerations into account. Where an act is shown to be ultra vires the effect is that it is void. Judicial control of administrative action is not only the part of administrative law which most interests lawyers. It is also, and more importantly, the ultimate safeguard for the ordinary citizen against unlawful action by what would otherwise appear to be the more powerful administration.

It is desirable at this stage to distinguish between appeal and review. An appeal consists of a rehearing of all or part of an issue which has already been dealt with at first instance, and results in the substitution for the original decision of a new decision, again upon all or part of the merits. Review, however, is far more basic, and involves the consideration by a court of some aspect of the original proceeding which may rob it of any validity or existence in law at all. The court must examine the fundamental point at issue, rather than any aspect of the merits of the case, and if satisfied that the complaint of the applicant is substantiated it will make an order which carries with it, either directly or by implication, acceptance of the argument that the whole proceeding below was void. It is in this context that the doctrine of ultra vires must be seen, for the assertion that an act is ultra vires is one of fundamental illegality.

The specific grounds for judicial control are basically three in number:

(1)   that the jurisdiction of the tribunal or other administrative authority was defective (the ultra vires doctrine);

(2)   that the authority acted in breach of natural justice. There are two distinct rules of natural justice, namely:

(a) that each interested party must have been heard, after being properly acquainted with any case that has been made against him; and

(b) that an authority must act in the absence of any reasonable suspicion that it was biased, or had any substantial personal, pecuniary or proprietary interest in a dispute before it;

(3)   that the authority acted in error of law. Some errors of law committed by, say, a tribunal may well go to jurisdiction, but it is also possible to be in error of law while nevertheless acting properly within jurisdiction. As we shall see in the next section of this chapter, it is possible to sue the Crown directly in tort, and in such cases also it would seem that the essential basis of the suit is that the Crown has acted in error of law.

The courts have made it clear that anything done ultra vires or in breach of natural justice is void, while an error of law within jurisdiction merely renders whatever has been done voidable, and thus needing to be quashed. It used to be thought that judicial control of administrative authorities was only possible where they were under a duty to act judicially, but the House of Lords decided in the important case of *Ridge v Baldwin*[1] in 1963 that the courts were free to examine any act by such an inferior authority, and to set it aside if one of the grounds for judicial review was established. In any event it has long been accepted that delegated legislation may be set aside if it should prove to be ultra vires.

In recent years the courts have been at some pains to describe the grounds for judicial control of action by administrative authorities in somewhat more modern terms, namely illegality, irrationality or procedural impropriety.[2] It can readily be seen that this in no sense amounts to any change of substance in the law, but it does perhaps explain more clearly what the legal rules mean. Illegality and irrationality between them cover the ultra vires doctrine in all its ramifications, including the unreasonable exercise of power, as well as error of law. Procedural impropriety covers the rules of natural justice. The courts have, however, also made clear that irrationality may not be used as a basis for attacking decisions with which the challenger or the court may disagree on the merits, for, as Lord Diplock explained, it applies only to a 'a decision which is so outrageous in its defiance of logic or of accepted moral standards that no sensible person who had applied his mind to the question to be decided could have arrived at it.'[3] Although the court will examine the reasons given by an inferior authority in order to see whether they offend against the rules just stated, it will not seek to impugn them merely because the judge might have taken a different view on the merits. Nevertheless an administrative body which is obliged to

1   [1964] AC 40, [1963] 2 All ER 66.
2   The founding of this new terminology was the speeches by the Law Lords in *Council of Civil Service Unions v Minister for the Civil Service* [1985] AC 374.
3   Ibid, at 410.

act fairly is usually under a general duty to give reasons for its decisions, and so if it fails to give reasons which are sufficient to show that it directed its mind to the relevant issues it will have acted in error of law.

With the growing importance within the United Kingdom of European laws, it is no surprise to find that our courts have now taken to developing administrative law by reference, from time to time, to European rules. The principle of proportionality (ie determining whether what was done was so bad in proportion to the whole issue at stake as to require to be struck down by the court) is used in European Community law, and modern court decisions in this country make some reference to it when considering whether or not action should be deemed irrational. Again the development of our administrative law on such issues as the general requirement to give reasons for decisions by an inferior authority has been influenced by the content of the European Convention on Human Rights.[4]

II REMEDIES

The actual remedies by which judicial control is achieved may be divided into two main groups, those which are direct and those which are indirect.

Direct remedies

The direct remedies in this field are primarily either appeals (provided by the statutes governing the various tribunals and other authorities) or actions for damages. But it should also be noted that a defence to a prosecution for an offence under delegated legislation may well take the form of an assertion that the regulation concerned is ultra vires. This, if successful, would be a particularly direct, albeit collateral, form of remedy.

It is not necessary to explain the nature of an appeal, and the identity of the courts or bodies to hear appeals from

4   See Chapter 7, above.

tribunals will depend upon the terms of the various statutes, but from most tribunals for which no appellate structure already existed the Tribunals and Inquiries Act 1992 (re-enacting a provision in the earlier 1958 Act) provides that an appeal on law lies direct to the High Court. Nor is it intended here to explain the elements of an action for damages which will lie wherever a tort has been committed or there has been a breach of contract. It is most unlikely that such an action would be appropriate against a tribunal not directly connected with the Crown, which can rarely be a party to a contract or commit a tort.

It may well be possible, however, that grounds for actions for damages may from time to time arise against ministers (sometimes deciding matters after inquiries) or other servants of the Crown. Until the passage of the Crown Proceedings Act 1947, actions in tort were not available against the Crown, and actions in contract could only be brought after a petition of right had been granted by the Crown itself, the petition having the effect of giving permission to the aggrieved person to bring his action. Some attention must therefore be accorded briefly to this statute and the resultant legal position.

THE CROWN PROCEEDINGS ACT 1947

Section 1 provides in effect that any person or body may bring an action in contract direct against a government department, except in three types of case. The exceptions are cases in which the Crown remains privileged from legal actions for damages, or for the recovery of a liquidated sum, or for injunction or specific performance, and cover contracts dependent upon a future grant of money from Parliament (for no litigant can be allowed to force Parliament to grant funds to enable the government to carry out its contractual obligations), contracts which fetter future executive action,[5] and contracts of service with

---

5   It is not really clear what this phrase means. There are very few direct cases upon the point: see J. D. B. Mitchell *The Contracts of Public Authorities* (1954); D. C. M. Yardley *Principles of Administrative Law* (2nd edn, 1986) Ch 5.

members of the armed forces.[6] Thus, to take an example from the last exception, no soldier has the right to sue the Crown for wrongful dismissal, or for reduction or arrears of pay. The reason for this is that the armed forces are still under the prerogative power of the Crown, as has been seen in Chapter 4, except in so far as funds for their upkeep, etc must be provided annually by Parliament.

Section 2 provides that actions in tort may now be brought directly against government departments or against the Crown as a whole, although only in specific circumstances, namely:

(1)   in respect of torts committed by its servants or agents;
(2)   in respect of any breach of duties which a person owed to his servants or agents at common law by reason of being their employer;
(3)   in respect of any breach of the duties attaching at common law to the ownership, occupation, possession or control of property; or
(4)   in respect of a breach by the Crown of statutory duties, even though the common law presumption that the Crown is not bound by statute is still applicable unless excluded by the statutes concerned expressly or by necessary intendment.

On reflection it is a little difficult to understand quite what this section was intended to mean, as it is hard to imagine the Crown committing any tort, except through a servant or agent, particularly since s 40 of the Act preserves the immunity of the monarch personally from any liability in law. But, whether by design or not, it seems plain that the true meaning of the section as enacted is to provide a general right of action in tort against the Crown wherever the Crown has been responsible for the commission of any tort whatever, except in specified instances set out in later

6   The position is now rather different in the case of contracts of service with civil servants. Modern legislation provides for a procedure before an Industrial Tribunal in cases of alleged unfair dismissal of employees, including Crown servants, and there is provision in suitable cases for an order of reinstatement or re-engagement, and for an award of compensation. But there is still no provision for action to be taken by civil servants against the Crown in the courts by traditional legal process.

sections. But any further consideration of the section must be deferred until the reader has consulted more detailed works upon the subject.[7] The common law personal liability of Crown servants of course remains untouched in any way by the Act. Such servants are personally liable for any injuries they commit for which they are unable to produce legal authority.

The remaining sections of the Act provide for certain special matters either not covered by the two general sections or exceptional to them. There is no need to examine them fully here, but in particular s 10 provided that the Crown was not liable for the death or personal injury of a member of the armed forces on duty caused by any other such member of the armed forces: the Admiralty Board or a Secretary of State could, if satisfied of the facts, issue a certificate that the persons concerned were on duty as members of the armed forces, and this certificate was final and could not be questioned in any court of law. This section of the 1947 Act has now been repealed by the Crown Proceedings (Armed Forces) Act 1987 (though not retrospectively), but there is provision for reactivating it in the event of any future war or grave national emergency. The Crown may now be ordered to produce documents relevant to any particular case (s 28 of the 1947 Act), although the privilege to withhold such documents where a minister certifies that their production might be injurious to the public interest is still left to the executive. 'Crown privilege', as it has usually been called, used to be accepted by the courts virtually without restriction, but in 1968 the House of Lords held that courts have the power to disallow any such claims of privilege, and to order the production of the documents concerned.[8] A court should not order the

---

7   See, eg, G. L. Williams *Crown Proceedings* (1948); H. Street *Governmental Liability* (1953); G. H. Treitel 'Crown Proceedings: Recent Developments' [1957] PL 321; and the textbooks and sourcebooks on administrative law.

8   *Conway v Rimmer* [1968] AC 910, [1968] 1 All ER 874. In *R v Lewes Justices, ex p Secretary of State for Home Department* [1973] AC 388 at 400, 406, 412, the House of Lords described the phrase Crown privilege as 'wrong', 'misleading', 'not accurate' and 'a misnomer', though in the event the claim to withhold from disclosure a confidential police report was allowed.

production of Cabinet minutes, or of documents the disclosure of which would be contrary to national security. But, subject to such judicial self-discipline, a court will now make a more objective inquiry into whether the public interest against disclosure outweighs the other public interest that in the administration of justice the eventual decision should be based on all the relevant facts. 'Public interest privilege' has in effect replaced the older 'Crown privilege'.[9]

Thus, although there are still exceptions and reservations, the Crown is now far nearer the position of a private contractor, employer or occupier of premises as far as litigation is concerned than it was before 1947. To this extent English law has approached more nearly to the concept of the rule of law favoured by Dicey, and discussed above in Chapter 7. In *M v Home Office*[10] the House of Lords held that ministers and civil servants are amenable to the court's contempt jurisdiction when acting in the discharge or purported discharge of their official duties. A citizen of Zaire had come to the United Kingdom seeking political asylum which was denied by the Home Office. Although his application for leave to apply for judicial review of the refusal was also refused, he made a fresh application and the judge postponed a decision on this for a day on the understanding from counsel for the Home Office that the applicant's deportation from the United Kingdom would be postponed overnight. In fact it had not been intended to give such an undertaking, and the applicant was deported on the personal decision of the Home Secretary. This was a contempt of court, and the Lords held that the Home Secretary in his personal capacity was rightly convicted for it, though no personal penalty was exacted from him. The full range of injunctions and other remedies was held to be available against the Crown and its servants.

9   See, eg, *Burmah Oil Co Ltd v Bank of England* [1980] AC 1090, [1979] 3 All ER 700.
10   [1993] 3 All ER 537.

Indirect remedies

THE PREROGATIVE ORDERS

Since the middle ages the superior courts of law (now the High Court in England) have possessed three methods of controlling the exercise of jurisdiction in inferior courts or bodies, and tribunals and inquiries of all kinds now come into the latter category. These methods of control were known as the prerogative writs, and their nature is essentially the same today, although their procedure was simplified by the Administration of Justice (Miscellaneous Provisions) Act 1938, s 7, so that they have now become prerogative orders. Each will be explained very shortly.

Certiorari

Any party who believes himself aggrieved by the proceedings of an administrative authority may apply to the High Court for a certiorari.

If any one of the alleged grounds for judicial control is proved to the satisfaction of the High Court, the proceeding below is quashed. Error of law on the face of the record of the inferior authority is no longer such a common ground for certiorari in practice as it was before direct appeals from most tribunals to the High Court on points of law were established by the Tribunals and Inquiries Act 1958 (now 1992), but it remains important for the review of cases decided by tribunals, such as Mental Health Review Tribunals, from which no such appeal yet lies. But it should be noted that no alternative decision on the merits is made by the High Court in a certiorari case, thus distinguishing the effect of this remedy from that of appeal.

Prohibition

This order is similar in most respects to certiorari, except that its effect, if granted, is to prevent a case from being heard or continuing before, say, a tribunal, rather than to quash what has already taken place. Thus it is sought at an earlier stage in the proceedings before the tribunal, but the grounds for its issue are similar, even though it is rare, if possible at all, that an error of law can be alleged, because the record of the issue is not yet completed below.

Mandamus

Whereas the two previous orders are negative in effect, mandamus is positive, for if granted it has the effect of ordering the tribunal to do something. It may be sought, for example, where a tribunal has refused to hold a proper hearing, or where a minister has failed to carry out a public duty or exercise a discretion entrusted to him.[11] But it will not lie against the Crown, or against any servant of the Crown to order him to perform any duty owed exclusively to the Crown.

All three of these remedies are regarded as 'last resort' remedies, for it is possible that a statute may have laid down a method of appeal from the particular tribunal concerned, in which case that course must be followed to the dissatisfaction of one of the parties before a prerogative order may be granted. But appeal, unlike the prerogative orders, has never been a common law remedy, and so no appeal is possible unless it has been provided for by statutory authority. In 1993 however, the Law Commission embarked on a review of both judicial review and statutory appeals, and it has now recommended several measures to bring about a closer integration of the two.

OTHER INDIRECT REMEDIES

Declaration

A simple declaration of the law upon a particular point may sometimes be an appropriate remedy against an administrative authority. No declaration may be sought, however, unless the point at issue is a real, and not theoretical, one; and a possible drawback to the remedy is that there is no method whereby it may be enforced, since the issue before the court is not strictly a 'live' dispute. All other judgments may always be enforced by attachment

11   Eg in *Padfield v Minister of Agriculture, Fisheries and Food* [1968] AC 997, [1968] 1 All ER 694.

for contempt, but there is no direct method of coercing a party against whom a declaration has been obtained. It may be that disobedience would lead to a later direct action for damages or an injunction, in which the law would already have been decided and only the facts would have to be proved. In any case it is possible to obtain a declaration in conjunction with some other positive remedy, such as an award of damages or an injunction, and there appears to be no record of a case in which a declaration has been disobeyed. But a court has refused a declaration where such a non-coercive remedy would be ineffective, as where the complaint was not that a tribunal had acted ultra vires, in which case its decision would be a nullity, but merely that it had made an error of law within the confines of its jurisdiction, which has been held to make the decision voidable.[12] It would not be possible for such a tribunal to reopen the matter unless its original decision had been *quashed*.

Injunction

This remedy has the effect of forbidding the doing of something, as being illegal. Thus it in many ways substantially resembles prohibition, but it is not used so often against administrative tribunals. Its most common use in the field of administrative law is against so-called 'domestic tribunals', such as disciplinary committees (eg of the Jockey Club), which are set up for internal purposes within a profession or a club, rather than by statute, or against trade unions.[13]

APPLICATION FOR JUDICIAL REVIEW

It can readily be seen that English administrative law has included a veritable patchwork of remedies, and in the latter part of the twentieth century it was more and more thought by lawyers that the procedure for obtaining any one or more of these remedies should be reformed and

---

12   *Punton v Ministry of Pensions and National Insurance (No 2)* [1964] 1 All ER 448, [1964] 1 WLR 226.
13   Eg as was attempted in *Gouriet v Union of Post Office Workers* [1978] AC 435, [1977] 3 All ER 70.

simplified. A Report published in 1976 by the Law Commission, on Remedies in Administrative Law,[14] recommended a new procedure which was then substantially implemented by amendments to the Rules of the Supreme Court coming into effect in 1978, and ultimately given statutory force by the Supreme Court Act 1981.[15] It is now provided that any person considered by the court to have sufficient standing in a matter may, as an alternative to applying for an individual remedy only, make what is termed 'an application for judicial review'. In his application he may ask for certiorari, prohibition, mandamus, declaration or an injunction, or any combination of them. The application must normally be made to the Divisional Court of the Queen's Bench Division, which in its discretion may make such order as it thinks fit as a result, and may also award damages where appropriate, though it may refuse to grant any application that is unduly delayed. The new rules eliminate several procedural defects surrounding the old remedies, and in particular provide that where the relief sought is certiorari the High Court may remit the matter to the court, tribunal or authority below with a direction to reconsider it, and to decide the matter in accordance with the findings of the High Court.

These reforms have proved to be a significant improvement in administrative law, and applications for judicial review have virtually replaced the older procedure of applying for individual indirect remedies. This is especially so because the Rules themselves prescribe that in an administrative law case an application for one or more of the prerogative orders may now only be made by the new procedure; and the courts have in recent cases taken the view that applications for declarations and injunctions in administrative law cases should also be by the same route. In 1983 the House of Lords twice held[16] that all matters of public law may only properly be reviewed by means of the application for judicial review:

14   Cmnd 6407.
15   Order 53, printed in SI 1977 No 55.
16   *O'Reilly v Mackman* [1983] 2 AC 237; *Cocks v Thanet District Council* [1983] 2 AC 286.

to seek review by other means (such as by direct action started by a writ or by originating summons) would be an abuse of the process of the court. But later decisions have clarified this by showing that it may still be appropriate to attempt collateral challenge of a public law issue arising in other civil proceedings. For example, it remains open to a defendant in civil proceedings to challenge the validity of any order which forms the basis of the plaintiff's case against him.[17] Again a general practitioner, who sued his National Health Service Family Practitioner Committee for damages for breach of contract when they had reduced his basic practice allowance by 20% because they considered he was not devoting enough time to providing general medical services within the NHS, was held entitled to have a collateral claim for a declaration that they had acted unlawfully dealt with in the same proceedings because he was primarily seeking to enforce a private right.[18]

For all practical purposes, therefore, the application for judicial review has replaced the older individual indirect remedies in the field of public law litigation, though they remain distinct and intact in private law litigation, such as family law disputes; and public law remedies may still be sought in collateral issues in other civil proceedings. The independent Justice — All Souls Review of Administrative Law[19] has recommended that there should be no artificial barriers making it difficult for a person to obtain any remedy, and has outlined various procedural reforms to this end as desirable. Although the Review has not yet been acted upon, the Law Commission reported along somewhat similar lines late in 1994, and suggested detailed procedural changes, including abolition of the old Latin names for remedies. We may therefore expect further reform before long.

---

17 *Wandsworth LBC v Winder* [1985] AC 461.
18 *Roy v Kensington and Chelsea Family Practitioner Committee* [1992] 1 AC 624.
19 See Chapter 11, above.

174   *The Control of Power*

FURTHER READING

Sir William Wade *Administrative Law* (7th edn, 1994)
J. F. Garner *Administrative Law* (7th edn, 1989)
D. Foulkes *Administrative Law* (7th edn, 1990)
S. H. Bailey, B. L. Jones and A. Mowbray *Cases and Materials on Administrative Law* (2nd edn, 1992)
S. A. de Smith *Judicial Review of Administrative Action* (5th edn, by J. Jowell and Lord Woolf, 1994)
P. P. Craig *Administrative Law* (3rd edn, 1994)
P. Cane *An Introduction to Administrative law* (2nd edn, 1992)
C. T. Emery and B. Smythe *Judicial Review* (1986)
J. Beatson and M. H. Matthews *Administrative Law: Cases and Materials* (2nd edn, 1989)
R. J. F. Gordon *Judicial Review: Law and Procedure* (1985)
C. M. Lewis *Judicial Remedies in Public Law* (1992).

Chapter 13

Ombudsmen

There have always been some areas of administrative power or executive discretion which have remained immune from the possibility of judicial review. A decision made by an administrative officer which is within his lawful jurisdiction, and which is made neither in breach of natural justice nor in error of law may well therefore be valid, and of course technically reasonable, but nevertheless harsh, or delayed, or inadequately explained. Again, there are whole areas of executive discretion which have always been held to be immune from any type of judicial review. Examples are the discretion of the Crown to grant or refuse so-called political asylum to refugees, or the powers of local education authorities to make discretionary grants to certain types of students. In such cases the traditional remedy available to anyone who considers himself aggrieved has been to approach an MP, with a view to getting him to ask a question in the House of Commons of the responsible Minister, or to approach a local councillor in the hope that he will take the matter up and prevail upon those responsible to change their minds. Any such approach may well be backed up by letters to the press, or by the agitation of some pressure group, but its success is always bound to be problematical, and doubts would be likely to remain one way or the other as to the justice of the eventual outcome.

It was in response to this haphazard state of affairs that the movement first grew in the United Kingdom for the establishment of some form of extra-judicial channel for the consideration and possible remedy of complaints.

Special impetus to the movement was given by the notorious Crichel Down affair. Shortly before the Second World War certain land in Dorset, known as Crichel Down, had been acquired compulsorily on behalf of what was then known as the Air Ministry, a predecessor of part of the present Ministry of Defence. The transaction was perfectly legally executed under emergency legislation then in force, but an undertaking was given at the time to the owner from whom it was purchased that he would be given the chance to repurchase it if the Crown should subsequently have no further use for the land. After the war the Air Ministry did indeed have no further use for it, and it was passed to the Ministry of Agriculture, which in its turn let it be known that it was prepared to consider disposing of the land either by sale or by lease. The original pre-war owner was by then dead, but his son-in-law, one Lieutenant-Commander Marten, who with his wife was farming adjoining land which had not been compulsorily acquired, made a bid to purchase the land. This was not accepted, and Crichel Down was sold to the Commissioners of Crown Lands, who then selected another tenant for it. Commander Marten protested and persisted in his protests at his treatment, and eventually the Minister appointed Sir Andrew Clarke QC to conduct an inquiry into the affair. Sir Andrew's Report was published in 1954,[1] and contained serious criticisms of impropriety by several civil servants within the Ministry of Agriculture who had, without any apparent justification, formed an aversion for Commander Marten, and revealed in a series of internal minutes passed within the Ministry a determination to prevent Marten acquiring the land, regardless of the financial or moral merits of his claim. In the event there was a debate in the House of Commons; the Minister, Sir Thomas Dugdale, resigned; and the civil servants concerned were reprimanded and moved to other posts within the civil service.

But the Crichel Down affair did not rest there, for it was clear from Sir Andrew Clarke's Report that, however

1 Report of the 'Public Inquiry ordered by the Minister of Agriculture into the disposal of land at Crichel Down' (Cmnd 9176). Recent research has suggested that the Clarke Report was itself not entirely free from blemish in respect of objectivity, but this does not affect its main thrust or detract in any way from the chain of events it unleashed.

improper or undesirable the conduct of the civil servants,
it at no stage had been illegal. The undertaking given to
the original owner was no more than morally binding, and
in any case could be argued as not extending to his son-in-
law, even though Marten and his wife were still farming
the adjoining land inherited from the original owner of
Crichel Down. The Ministry, like any other lessor or
vendor, was entitled to dispose of its own property as it
thought fit. Thus Marten had no claim in law which he
could have prosecuted against the Ministry in any court
or tribunal.

Eventually the British section of the International
Commission of Jurists, JUSTICE, set up an independent
committee under the chairmanship of a former Chief
Justice of Singapore, Sir John Whyatt, to investigate the
Scandinavian institution of the 'Ombudsman', and the
report of this committee, often known as the Whyatt
Report,[2] was published in 1961. There is no completely
satisfactory English translation of the word ombudsman,
but it has been variously rendered as 'complaints officer',
'commissioner' or (in countries like Spain and Portugal)
'defender of the people'. The first ombudsman appeared in
Sweden in 1809, though the full powers of the Swedish
Ombudsman, which included the right to institute
prosecutions, including prosecutions against judges, have
not been copied by many of those countries in the present
century which have instituted ombudsmen. The first
twentieth century ombudsman office was set up in 1919
in Finland, and the next was in Denmark in 1954, and it
was this latter ombudsman institution which particularly
influenced the findings of the Whyatt Report, for the
Danish Ombudsman is an officer of Parliament with wide
powers of investigation, but relying upon his prestige and
influence to achieve results, rather than any positive
executive authority. The first Commonwealth country to
borrow from the Scandinavian experience was New
Zealand by the Parliamentary Commissioner (Ombudsman) Act 1962, but the Whyatt Report had its effect in
the United Kingdom, after prolonged debate both within

2   'The Citizen and the Administration: the Redress of Grievances'.

and outside Parliament, when the first British Ombudsman was established in 1967.

I THE PARLIAMENTARY COMMISSIONER FOR ADMINISTRATION

The Parliamentary Commissioner Act 1967[3] created the office of Parliamentary Commissioner for Administration, now commonly known as the Parliamentary Ombudsman. The Commissioner is appointed by the Crown, and holds office until the age of 65, being otherwise removable only in consequence of an address from both Houses of Parliament, or for incapacity on medical grounds, so that his tenure of office is protected in the same way as that of superior judges. Doubtless in the interests of co-operation he is an *ex officio* member of the Council on Tribunals. He may investigate any action taken by or on behalf of a government department or other listed authority, provided that there is no court or tribunal in which such action may reasonably be challenged, though his investigation can only be set in motion as a result of the receipt of a complaint that there has been maladministration. There is, however, a set process prescribed by the Act for the reference of such complaints.

The complaint must be in writing, it must be made by someone resident in the United Kingdom who claims to have sustained injustice in consequence of the maladministration, and it must be made in the first place to an MP within 12 months of the person aggrieved first having notice of the matters alleged in the complaint (though the Ombudsman may conduct an investigation pursuant to a complaint not made within that period if he considers there are special circumstances which make it proper to do so). It is then for the MP to refer it to the Ombudsman, with the consent of the complainant, and with a request that the Ombudsman conduct an

---

3   Amended by the Parliamentary and Health Service Commissioners Act 1987, which extended the jurisdiction of the Parliamentary Commissioner to a long list of quangos (quasi-autonomous non-governmental organisations).

investigation into it. This 'filter' of complaints through MPs has always been controversial, but its purpose was closely related to the fear that the Ombudsman might be swamped with complaints unless some effort were made to intercept some of the more eccentric or worthless complaints before they should reach him. This fear has not been borne out by events, for the Parliamentary Ombudsman usually receives less than 1,000 complaints a year (a caseload of only about one-fifth that carried by each of the English Local Government Ombudsmen who will be referred to presently), and it is still possible that in due course the 'MP filter' will be removed.

The Ombudsman must conduct his investigations in private, and the procedure he adopts is left to his own discretion. But his power to investigate is much strengthened by his right to require any minister, officer or member of a department or authority concerned, or indeed anyone else, to furnish information or produce documents relevant to his investigation. He has the same powers as a court to compel the attendance and examination of witnesses; and the Crown is specifically not entitled to attempt to shelter behind any claim of Crown privilege in respect of the production of documents or the giving of evidence. It is noteworthy that this statutory provision preceded the House of Lords' decision in *Conway v Rimmer*, discussed in Chapter 12, by a year. On the other hand information concerning the proceedings of the Cabinet or any of its committees is understandably exempt from the Ombudsman's jurisdiction. At the conclusion of any investigation he must send to the MP who requested it a report of the results of his investigation, or a statement of his reasons for deciding not to conduct it. A similar report must go to the initial complainant, and to the principal officer of the department or authority concerned. He may make a special report to each House of Parliament, but in any event must make an Annual Report to Parliament upon his work. It has always been the practice of the House of Commons to refer all such reports to their Select Committee on the Parliamentary Commissioner for consideration and comment; and the Ombudsman has himself established it as his own normal practice to send all his reports upon investigations to this Select Committee.

One patent difficulty produced by the Act is that it nowhere defines 'maladministration', the one quality in an administrator which under the Act should cause an adverse report to be made by the Ombudsman. This may seem a curious omission by Parliament, but in fact it was by design, for Mr Richard Crossman, the minister who at the time was steering the Bill through the House of Commons, stated that it was believed it would be better for the Ombudsman to work out for himself the boundaries of maladministration, a concept which was hitherto unknown in the United Kingdom. Mr Crossman did however say that he would expect the term to include bias, neglect, inattention, delay, incompetence, ineptitude, perversity, turpitude and arbitrariness, and these words have always been referred to since then as the 'Crossman catalogue'. Yet they have formed only the starting point in the development of the work of the Ombudsman, who is concerned really with the whole flavour of administrative action, and will judge whether in all the circumstances of any matter coming before him the administrative authority acted reasonably. Thus he will test the whole quality of the administrative action and its effect upon the citizen. Nevertheless it may be remembered that the commonest type of maladministration found by the Parliamentary Ombudsman, and also by the other United Kingdom ombudsmen who will be mentioned presently, is unnecessary delay, a fault which is more usually inadvertent than intentional.

II OTHER UNITED KINGDOM OMBUDSMEN

It was recognised very soon after the creation of the institution of the Parliamentary Ombudsman that this might be only the first step along the road towards a wider scope for extra-judicial remedies against the administration, and this very soon proved to be the case. The Parliamentary Commissioner Act 1967 was drafted in restrictive terms which may not be all that surprising for a statute designed to institute an entirely new approach to the provision of remedies. The 'MP filter' is only the most obvious of the restrictions imposed upon the Ombudsman's powers, yet perhaps the most unexpected effect of the Act was to give him jurisdiction over complaints against what is now called the Department of Health (in 1967 the Ministry of Health), but to deny him jurisdiction over the whole of the hospital service. It rapidly became clear that this lacuna could not be allowed to last, and when the Health Service was reorganised a few years later the gap was plugged. Three Health Service Commissioners were appointed, one each for England, Wales and Scotland, with a duty to investigate any alleged failure in a service provided by a health authority, or any action taken by or on behalf of such an authority, where there is a complaint of injustice in consequence of maladministration.

The procedure to be followed by the three Commissioners is similar to that laid down for the Parliamentary Ombudsman, save that a complainant need not channel his complaint through an MP, and may approach a Commissioner direct. Reports by the Commissioners must be made to Parliament, and are in fact received by the same Select Committee of the Commons which receives the Parliamentary Ombudsman's reports. All three posts have since their inception been held by the same person who for the time being is the Parliamentary Commissioner for Administration, and the net effect has been that the existence and powers of the Health Service Ombudsman amount in reality to an extension of the previously unduly restrictive provisions for the Parliamentary Ombudsman.

As part of the very strong pressure which had been exerted after the 1967 Act for extension and improvement of the ombudsman principle there was a movement for a similar mechanism in the field of local government, which will itself be the subject of the next and final chapter of this book. It was argued that, if there was any maladministration in central government departments with their generally high standards of civil service morality, it was even more likely that maladministration would be found in local government, which would be largely unaffected by the strength of the civil service tradition.

Accordingly the Local Government Act 1974 established two Commissions for Local Administration, one for England and the other for Wales, and the Local Government (Scotland) Act 1975 established a similar Commissioner (though not a Commission) for Scotland. The 1974 Act does not specify how many Commissioners there should be, but in fact there have always so far been three appointed to hold office at the same time in the English Commission, while only one Commissioner has been required for Wales. This is not surprising because the caseload for the English Commission, covering a population in the region of 48 millions, is so much greater than that for the Welsh Commission, dealing with a population under 3 millions. All these Commissioners are now generally known as Local Government Ombudsmen. The English Local Government Ombudsmen divide up their work between them on a geographical basis, and currently maintain offices in London, York and Coventry. For reasons of co-operation the Parliamentary Ombudsman is an *ex officio* member of both the English and Welsh Commissions, but in fact all the public sector ombudsmen maintain close contact with each other in practice. The final pattern of these ombudsmen is completed by the existence of a separate Northern Ireland Parliamentary Commissioner and also a Commissioner for Complaints, both offices having been held in recent years by the same appointee.

The various Local Government Ombudsmen have jurisdiction to consider complaints of injustice caused by the maladministration of local authorities and certain other related bodies. Complaints must be in writing, but the provisions in the 1974 and 1975 legislation making it necessary for complaints to be made through members of the authorities complained about have since been removed, so that the ombudsmen may now receive complaints direct from the complainants. The great majority of complaints are now made direct, and this has been one of the factors instrumental in the marked increase in the numbers of complaints to all public sector ombudsmen over the years, with the single exception of the Parliamentary Ombudsman. For example, the Commission for Local

Administration in England received nearly 13,500 complaints in the year from April 1992 to March 1993, about five times the number it had to deal with ten years before. If and when the 'MP filter' to the Parliamentary Ombudsman is removed it can be anticipated that there will be an increase in his caseload also, though as with other ombudsmen it will not necessarily mean that more of the complaints will in the end turn out to be justified.

To this pattern of ombudsmen in the public sector have now been added, since 1990, two Legal Services Ombudsmen, one for England and Wales and the other for Scotland, whose task is to investigate the way the legal professions deal with complaints against them by the public. The Police Complaints Authority, established in 1984, and which has already been mentioned in Chapter 4, bears some resemblance to the avenues for extra-judicial remedy being considered in this chapter, though it lacks a fully independent method of investigating complaints against the police. Other fairly similar bodies include the Broadcasting Complaints Commission and the Prisons Ombudsman. In the private sector there are now a number of ombudsmen set up by professions or sections of the business community, or in a few cases by statute, and they include the Banking Ombudsman, Insurance Ombudsman, Building Societies Ombudsman, Pensions Ombudsman and the Corporate Estate Agents Ombudsman.

III OMBUDSMEN IN PRACTICE

Broadly it can be said that ombudsmen have proved to be highly successful in achieving the remedies they seek. Unlike judges they do not have the power to enforce their decisions directly, and their reports are recommendations rather than binding judgments. With the exception of some of the private sector ombudsmen, who are much assisted by the voluntary agreements of their founding professions or businesses that they will hold themselves bound by any ombudsman award up to a certain maximum sum of money, ombudsmen must rely upon their powers of persuasion to achieve results. They are helped by their well respected position, and by the strong sense of justice which certainly persists in public life. The Parliamentary Ombudsman is greatly assisted by the Select Committee of the Commons which is always keen to see that his recommended remedies are achieved. The Local Government Ombudsmen do not have such clear assistance. They report their findings to the complainant and to the authority complained about, but do not have any direct help in achieving their objectives from Parliament or any other outside body. Nevertheless their legislation makes some provision for the use of notices in local newspapers, and the high profile of local, and occasionally national, media coverage has helped to persuade reluctant councils to comply with recommendations. On occasion the ombudsman recommendations are not implemented in full, but on the whole this is a sufficiently rare occurrence for it not to detract seriously from the effectiveness of the system.

The majority of ombudsman cases are concerned with comparatively minor matters, such as delay in assessing tax liability, failure to repair a council flat adequately, or the failure to follow the normal internal procedure in dealing with a planning application. But sometimes the issue may be more far-reaching or involve a significant sum of money. A celebrated case involved the Parliamentary Ombudsman's investigation of the actions of the Department of Trade and Industry in relation to the regulation of a brokerage business known as Barlow Clowes, which had subsequently collapsed to the detriment of large numbers of small investors in the securities they offered. The Ombudsman found the Department's monitoring of the business to have been inadequate, and that this was maladministration which had caused injustice to the investors. He reported this to Parliament in 1989, and the Secretary of State for Trade and Industry announced in the House of Commons that he and his Department disagreed with the Ombudsman, but that 'as a mark of respect for his office' the Department would nevertheless pay out about £150 million in compensation to the investors. This large sum was about 90% of the total losses found by the Ombudsman as injustice. Not only did this substantially satisfy the determination made by the Ombudsman, but it provided a powerful example of how effective the ombudsman process can be.

Further developments of the ombudsman system can be expected in course of time. The Justice — All Souls Review of Administrative Law, published in 1988 (and referred to above in Chapters 11 and 12), recommended particularly that principles of good administration should be drawn up, and that this work should be carried out by the Parliamentary Ombudsman. In the event the task was given, by the Local Government and Housing Act 1989, to the Local Government Ombudsmen who, starting in 1992, have been publishing a series of practice guidance notes for local government, one of which is of central significance and entitled Good Administrative Practice. With effect from 1994 the Parliamentary, Health Service and Local Government Ombudsmen have been given the task of monitoring a new freedom of information policy, and in course of time this may well increase the caseloads that they bear.

From time to time there have been suggestions that all the public sector ombudsmen should be combined in a single commission for public administration or similar body. But co-operation between all the ombudsmen is so well developed, including provision for forwarding complaints sent to the wrong office on to the correct one, that it is hard to see what would be achieved by this. The present ombudsmen have specialist functions and subjects which are probably well enough understood, and developing or reforming legislation is constantly considered and enacted as necessary.

The Maastricht Treaty, referred to in Chapter 2, makes provision for the creation of a European Community Ombudsman whose task will be to investigate complaints of injustice caused by maladministration of the EC authorities. Now that the Treaty has been ratified by all the current member states of the Community the office is expected to be set up during 1995, but the new Community Ombudsman will not of course have any jurisdiction over matters now falling under the ombudsmen in the United

Kingdom, still less any powers over those existing Parliamentary or Local Government Ombudsmen.

FURTHER READING

F. Stacey *The British Ombudsman* (1971)
R. Gregory and P. Hutchesson *The Parliamentary Ombudsman* (1975)
M. Seneviratne *Ombudsmen in the Public Sector* (1994)
N. Lewis and P. Birkinshaw *When Citizens Complain: Reforming Justice and Administration* (1993)
Publications of the International Ombudsman Institute, Alberta, Canada.

Chapter 14

Local Government

The machinery for the government of local areas throughout the United Kingdom is almost entirely separate from that of the central government, though always subject to the overriding powers of Parliament by statute or, where appropriate, of the central government. It is of course possible and proper for the government of the whole country to exercise such powers as it possesses by virtue of Acts of Parliament or the royal prerogative in such a way as to affect local areas of the Kingdom in various different ways. But, subject to such exercise of power, the different local authorities are independently empowered to carry out and enforce executive duties within their particular districts. They may also legislate upon certain matters within their jurisdiction, and all these powers are derived either from Acts of Parliament or from Royal Charters granted under the royal prerogative.[1] The exercise of the prerogative in this field is regulated by statute, and the powers of local authorities are mostly contained in the London Government Act 1963 and the Local Government Act 1972, as amended, and the Local Government Finance Act 1992. But it should be noted that provisions for further structural change of local government authorities throughout Great Britain have now been enacted, and are due to be implemented within a few years. For example, the Local Government Act 1992 established a Local Government Commission to review the local authorities in England outside Greater London and

---

1   And see Chapters 4 and 10, above.

to recommend structural, boundary or electoral changes which may then be brought into effect by the Secretary of State for the Environment with or without modification. It is currently expected that the review will be completed by 1995, and that changes will be implemented in stages by 1997. A number of authorities are expected in future to become single-tier or all-purpose. It is our purpose in this chapter to outline the types of local authorities which exist at the present time, and their various powers.

The authorities listed below are those which currently exist in England, all of which are under the general supervision of the Secretary of State for the Environment, although this does not mean that he necessarily wields great arbitrary powers over them. The local authorities in Northern Ireland are not dissimilar in the main, and elections for the present Northern Ireland district councils were first held in 1973. They are under the supervision of the Secretary of State for Northern Ireland. New single-tier authorities in Wales and Scotland are due to begin their work in 1995 and 1996 respectively, supervised by the Secretaries of State for Wales and Scotland. It may be noted that, in Northern Ireland, elections for the district councils and for the European Parliament (as a result of the European Assembly Elections Act 1978) are held by proportional representation, ie members of political parties are elected in similar proportion to that of the votes cast. Elsewhere in the United Kingdom all elections are conducted according to the principle that the winner is whichever candidate receives the most votes.

I THE TYPES OF LOCAL AUTHORITIES

The local authorities of England and Wales may be divided up as follows.

THE LOCAL AUTHORITIES OF LONDON

The local government organisation in the London area was reorganised by the London Government Act 1963 and the Local Government Acts 1985 and 1988. Greater London consists of the City of London, the 32 London Boroughs, the Inner Temple and the Middle Temple. It includes areas which were previously part of surrounding counties, but it is possible that the Act of 1963 does not go far enough, in that it fails to take account of large areas in surrounding counties where many working Londoners live. The authorities of Greater London are as follows.

London Borough Councils

There is one council for each of the London Boroughs, and each consists of a mayor and councillors. The mayor is elected annually by the council, and the councillors are elected every four years. The powers of these councils, like those of the metropolitan district councils, discussed below, are for most local government matters all-purpose.

The City of London Corporation

This body corporate came into being as a result of prescription over a long period of history but its powers have been regulated from time to time by Royal Charters and by statutes. It may be regarded as roughly of parallel status to the London Borough Councils, and its functions are exactly the same. The government of the corporation is carried on through three 'Courts' or councils, the Court of Common Council, the Court of Common Hall and the Court of Aldermen. It is not necessary here to consider further their exact functions or composition, but the various representatives who sit in these Courts are the Lord Mayor of London, aldermen, common councilmen, and two Sheriffs and certain liverymen of the ancient City Companies of craftsmen and tradesmen.

The Benchers of the Inner and Middle Temples

Certain minor local government functions are still exercised by the Benchers of these two Inns of Court, and the London Government Acts 1939 and 1963 recognise that the Temples are within Greater London, but outside the City and the London Boroughs. This is a traditional status, for which there appears to be no real legal foundation,

other than prescription or custom,[2] but it is of little
importance in practice, as the inhabitants of the area are
nearly all barristers in their chambers, very few of whom
actually reside in the Temple.

In addition to the authorities so far listed, there are a
number of separate authorities administering services
which, outside London, are sometimes the concern of local
authorities. These include the Port of London Authority
and the London Regional Transport Board. There are also
certain joint boards responsible for fire and civil defence,
and (outside Greater London) the police.

LOCAL AUTHORITIES OUTSIDE LONDON

Outside London the structure of local authorities is
uniform and governed by the Local Government Acts 1972
and 1985, but it is likely to be considerably affected in the
near future under the provisions of the Local Government
Act 1992, mentioned above. The present authorities were
elected for the first time in 1973, and took over their full
powers on 1 April 1974. In effect most of the country is for
local government purposes covered by a three-tier system
of authorities, governing respectively counties, districts
and parishes. But six of the counties are designated as
metropolitan counties, because they cover areas of the
greatest concentration of population and industry, such as
the West Midlands and Merseyside. In these counties there
are no county councils; instead the metropolitan district
councils have greater powers than those in non-
metropolitan districts because they are virtually all-
purpose. The three types of authorities are as follows.

Non-metropolitan county councils

Each council consists of a chairman and councillors, all of
whom are elected for four years, and all of whom retire at
the same time. The last election for these councils was in
May 1993. Each council has a number of powers exercised
concurrently with district councils, such as the control of

2   But see Williamson *The History of the Temple, London* for further
information.

museums and art galleries, swimming baths, parks and open spaces, tree preservation, and many aspects of town development. But the county council has exclusive powers over such matters as structure plans for the county, highways, traffic, consumer protection, refuse disposal, education, youth employment, personal social services and libraries.

District councils

Each county is divided into a number of districts, each of which has its own council, consisting of a chairman and councillors. Each member is elected for four years, but normally one-third of the council will retire every year, except for a year in which a county council election is to be held. Any district council or London Borough Council may, however, opt for the whole council to be elected together every four years, and many districts, including all the London Boroughs, have so opted. As well as the powers exercised concurrently with county councils, non-metropolitan district councils have exclusive powers over such matters as housing, planning development control, building regulations, markets and fairs, local licensing, refuse collection, clean air and home safety. Metropolitan district councils have virtually exclusive powers over most matters of local government concern, including education, youth employment, personal social services and libraries.

Parish councils and meetings

All parishes in rural areas have parish meetings, which consist of a chairman and all the local government electors of the parish, and which must meet at least once a year. Such parishes with a population of 300 or more must also have a parish council (and parishes with a population of under 300 may elect to have a parish council), consisting of a chairman, elected annually, and councillors, elected for four years and retiring in rotation. A council has slightly greater powers than a meeting, but the powers of each cover such subjects as the maintenance and signposting of footpaths and bridleways, and parks and open spaces.

In all these authorities, except parish meetings, members are directly elected by the people. But councils have the power to recognise service to local government by conferring the title of 'honorary alderman' upon suitable persons. Non-elected members may be co-opted to committees. Special provisions enable any district council for an area which was previously a borough by Royal Charter to retain its previous status, together with the title of mayor for its chairman. Similarly a petition may be submitted, and will be favourably considered, to enable any district to retain any special distinction or title, such as 'Royal Borough', 'City', 'Lord Mayor' or 'Sheriff'.

Of more fundamental importance, the Local Government Act 1972 and Local Government (Access to Information) Act 1985 extend the rights of the public and press to attend council meetings and meetings of all committees and sub-committees of local authorities, and to inspect certain council documents. Councillors now receive a taxable flat-rate attendance allowance when on council business.

It will be seen from the above that the local administration of each part of England and Wales is accounted for by at least one locally elected authority, none of which is a national body. But the central government does have certain supervisory powers over these authorities, which are conferred by Act of Parliament. It is not necessary here to examine the supervisory powers closely, for they are of different kinds created under different statutes, but primarily this control exists because all local authorities receive financial grants from the Treasury to supplement their own local income (raised partly by rents and other commercial undertakings, and partly by the council tax which, under the Local Government Finance Act 1992, replaced the former community charge and, before that, general rates), and to pay for such local administration as cannot be afforded by the local funds. It is therefore easy to appreciate that the government will only initiate or support legislation in Parliament to provide for such financial grants when the local authorities affected have behaved in a proper manner in the immediate past, and seem likely to continue to do so. Sometimes the Secretary of State is empowered to make discretionary grants or to supervise the local authorities in certain ways according to his discretion, and then the exercise of such discretion will depend even more upon the 'good behaviour' of the authorities concerned, but in certain ways the 1972 Act has provided local authorities with greater financial freedom than hitherto. It can also be seen that, just as Parliament is able to control the functions and even the existence of local authorities by virtue of its legislative supremacy,[3] so it may also delegate powers of administration or legislation to the central government and to the local government authorities.[4] The powers of the latter are both administrative and legislative, with the restrictions discussed already in Chapter 10.

It is not proposed to discuss further in this chapter the powers of local authorities over the police, upon which the reader will find an account in Chapter 4 above. There is also no need to deal specifically with the powers to create committees or appoint officers (such as Chief Executive Officers), all of which depend on their governing legislation.

II WHO ELECTS MEMBERS OF LOCAL AUTHORITIES?

Since the Representation of the People Act 1949, now replaced by the Representation of the People Act 1983, the franchise for local government elections has been practically equated to that existing for Parliamentary elections, even though it is not quite identical. The right to vote is possessed by all European Community citizens of full age who are (1) not subject to any legal incapacity,[5] and (2) either resident in the area on the qualifying date,[6] or, if not so resident, who occupy land or premises in the area as owners or tenants. Thus there is an alternative

3   See Chapter 2, above.
4   See Chapter 10, above.
5   See Chapter 3, above. The legal incapacities are the same as for national elections, save that peers may vote in local elections.
6   10 October in each year, the annual register of electors being published the following 15 February: Electoral Registers Act 1953.

occupation qualification for those who cannot satisfy the residence qualification. Peers also have the right to vote in local elections.

Since the local government reorganisation of the past 25 years, party politics have come to play almost as great a part in local government elections as they do in national elections, and most candidates for election now stand as party candidates. In many ways the growth of the party political element in local government may seem to be regrettable, since the problems for any administrative sub-division of the country are practical everyday ones rather than questions of national importance, and there are all too many examples of experienced and hard-working local councillors who lose their seats solely because of the temporary swing of the political pendulum against their own party. But on the other hand social policy is bound to play a certain part in the duties of such authorities, and there are advantages in groups of council members having a worked-out and agreed policy on such issues. It is of course important that the size of grants to local authorities from the Exchequer is not influenced to any measurable extent by the political bias of the central government in relation to local authorities dominated by members of their own or an opposition party, and on the whole confidence in this can be safely maintained.

FURTHER READING

S. Bailey *Cross on Principles of Local Government Law* (1992)
K. Davies *Local Government Law* (1983)
Lord Redcliffe-Maud and B. Wood *English Local Government Reformed* (1974).

Index